Vibrating To Spirit

A Psychic's Journey To The Other Side

Kathleen Tucci

Intuitive Psychic / Dallas, Texas

Vibrating To Spirit – A Psychic's Journey To The Other Side

PRINTING HISTORY
Third printing paperback edition / August 2006

This book is an Intuitive Psychic publication and is available at special quantity discounts for bulk purchases for sales promotions, premiums, fund-raising, or educational use. Special books, or book excerpts, can also be created to fit specific needs. For details, write:

Unique Markets / Kathleen Tucci
5512 Charleston Drive
Frisco, Texas 75035

World Wide Web site address is
http://www.kathleentucci.com

ISBN 0-9728973-0-5

PRINTED IN THE UNITED STATES OF AMERICA

To my loving husband Lou, whose everlasting encouragement and willingness to love unconditionally has made me a better person in the world. I will love you always!

Contents

Acknowledgements

My sincere and heartfelt thanks go out to all of the families and their loved ones in spirit who allowed me to share their fascinating and deeply moving stories so that I might inspire others to know the captivating and evidential proof that life does go on.

To my parents, Burton and Mary: Thank you for instilling in me a powerful foundation and belief system in God in building my life. Your emotional strength by which you live your lives has proven to be an integral part of my learning by watching, and that unconditional love can accomplish miraculous results when blended with intelligence in knowing what a soul truly needs. Thank you for showing me how much abundant compassion allows you to change the world.

To my mother-in-law, Helen: Thank you for becoming my rock of Gibraltar. Your unwavering enthusiasm and commitment to my work and this book has not only provided me with a tremendous sense of support but also the desire to forge ahead when my spirit was tired and weak. Your energy and empowering love is a large part of the reason this book exists and I am forever grateful God put such a delightful, compassionate and wise beacon of spiritual light in my life…you!

To my sister, Cynthia and two brothers, Shawn and Tim: Thank you for always being there for me and for your total and absolute love.

To my grandparents, Karl and Claudia: Thank you for inspiring me early on to believe in myself, in my God, and in my fellow man regardless of what obstacles might come my way. I give you my deepest gratitude for continuing to educate me as much from the other side as you did here on the earthly plane. The bonds of our love will keep us connected until I see you again.

To my great-grandmother, Lena: You are still after 30 years, as sadly missed as the day you joined our Maker in heaven. Thank you for always protecting me and for guiding me in the right direction. I await the blessed day when I can be in your arms once more.

To my grandparents, Bill and May: Thank you for teaching me only things your souls could have provided. You showed me that each one us possesses the ability to make an important contribution.

To my children, LoriAnn, Stacy, Brock, Heather, Joe and Chris: The love we share and the laughter which is our medicine is the glue that holds this family so tightly together. Like the colors in the rainbow, you are a magnificent prism in my life.

To Doreen: Your close friendship and endless dedication to make lemons into lemonade has inspired me to know the true limitlessness of the human spirit! You continue to teach me new ways to love and how to see the forest through the trees.

To my son-in-law, Brian: A shining pearl in a deep dark sea; your love brightens my existence. Fortunate to have you as part of our family, we have been richly blessed!

To Jean: For all your love, your extreme wisdom and your guided encouragement which helped to make this book a reality, I am forever grateful. Thanks for always being there and for being the best friend one can ask for.

To Mike, Molly and Jody: Thank you for always accepting me for who I am and for showing me through our deep and trusted friendship what it means to truly have soul mates by your side.

To Aunt Anne, Paul, Grandma Anna, and Baron: To the teaching souls who connected many of the dots for me. Thank you for your love from the other side and your help in answering so many questions about life in spirit.

To Tasos Kostas and Dan O'Malley of 'The Dan and Tasos Show' at KLLI Radio in Dallas: Thank you for your friendship and support in providing me with a venue to express my beliefs and help educate the masses that life is ever-lasting. Your sincerity towards my work is appreciated and I will always treasure the great laughs and memories you've given me through our on-air adventures. Comrades forever!

To Tonya and Erika: Thank you for being in my life and for giving me things which I can never repay. May the love and care you show to others be returned to you ten-fold!

To Barbara and Rita: Thank you for your generosity and support in my work and for believing in me, helping me to spread the word that life is eternal.

To Marco and Miranda: Thank you for adding so much color and love to my life. I am grateful for your companionship and look forward to what we will discover in our continued spiritual journey together.

To Susan and Chris: "Two may talk under the same roof for many years, yet never really know each other; and two others at first speech are old friends." From the moment we met divine intervention was at play and I knew instantly ours would be a friendship which would last forever! Thank you for filling my life with laughter, joy and the continuing discovery of how love shapes lives.

To the rest of my family and friends: You have all been a part of this project in one fashion or another. Know that I love you deeply and offer my many thanks for how you have all helped touch, shape, form, and added to the puzzle of my existence.

Preface

As a child, the world is an awe-inspiring playground. Adventures are things that occur on a daily basis, learning the ins and outs of existence in this earthly plane. I remember very vividly an experience I had one evening when I was seven. Lying in bed before drifting to sleep I saw what looked like a movie playing in my head. Images and visions of people I did not know seemingly racing around feverishly back and forth. As if this film projecting in my mind was on fast-forward. I remember thinking to myself, "Why don't they slow down, at least then maybe I could make sense of what it was I was seeing." But the more I wanted it to slow down, the faster it raced. People's faces flying into my line of sight, stopping, looking at me, and then whisking away as fast as they came. I could feel them spinning around me, as if dancing this wild ritual yet to no apparent rhythm. Just darting about again and again, houses, rooms, and scenes I was unfamiliar with rushing past me. Gratefully after some time, the images seemed to settle down and melt away, and thankful, I fell asleep.

In trying to explain to those around me the next day, my elusive yet poignant experience, they surmised the rationalization I must be feverish and was delusional. In other words..."It's just your imagination." It wouldn't be until thirty years later when, through a bizarre series of events, I would come to realize those racy episodes were in fact not hallucinations or my imagination working overtime, but my ability to connect with another realm of existence – I was literally vibrating to spirit!

Forward

My interest in psychic abilities has spanned decades. I've read just about every book I can find regarding the paranormal. What makes this book so wonderful is the author's open and honest writing style. She has seen her share of hardships and loss. Perhaps this is why she is so very conscious of the grief of others and so passionately works to connect her clients and readers with their loved ones on the other side.

Tucci's compassion is apparent with every word she writes. Woven among personal recollections of how she found her gift, the author recounts several of the readings she has done for people over the years. Many are brought comfort by seeing the proof that only someone of Kathleen's talent could bring to bear. Tucci is transforming lives with her loving work with others. There are more than seven chapters in this book crammed full of simple exercises, instructions and advice for those wanting to connect to the other side. Again, the material is clear, concise and accessible to all.

- Jeni Mayer, Managing editor of *Body Mind Spirit Magazine* and
author of *Suspicion Island* and *The Mystery of the Missing Will*

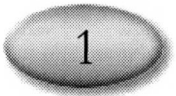

~ *A Gift Unnoticed* ~

Sitting in the pew on Sunday morning, I could feel God's light and love shining in through the tall obelisk stain glass windows of the church my great-great-grandfather built. I always felt so secure there. On many occasions I would day dream during church service and find myself on intriguing quests. Letting my mind wander, I would meet up with acquaintances and visit far away places I sensed a connection to. Looking back, I realize now I was practicing visualization exercises and was meditating in a semi-trance state. I was just too young to understand what I was really experiencing. Growing up in the Lutheran faith taught me that although I was to fear God, He was also a loving and forgiving power who knew I was a sinner. Be sorry for my sins, be a good Christian, repent and I was guaranteed heaven. My mom was raised Catholic. When she married my father she decided to convert to Lutheran so they could worship together. Funny, I would later in life, being raised Lutheran, marry a Catholic and practice Catholicism to worship with my husband.

For a couple of summers during my teens college kids would reside at our home, on loan to us from the various Christian schools in Wisconsin. They would hang out throughout the summer season to run Vacation Bible School. I would sit in our back yard with about twelve to fifteen other kids and sing Kumbiya while someone strummed an acoustic guitar. Long hair, sandals, a burlap bag, and you were all set. Those days were very carefree. I am the oldest of four children. My parents, who were firm believers in hard work and little play, not only kept us out of trouble but also kept our focus on what was important in life. They were right. My childhood was relatively pain free, and probably very dreamy compared to most. We always had food on the table, never really wanted for much of anything, and always felt a deep sense of family and structure. Grounding if you will, that made you know you were a part of something great!

There was really only two times in my childhood that I can recount as ever having to deal with major trauma. When my great-grandmother Lena passed when I was twelve, and then eight years later when my grandfather Karl died. They would each play a significant role in my life. Through Lena I would experience for the first time the true pain suffered in the loss of a loved one. On the other end of the spectrum, through Karl, I would learn *dead is not really dead.*

Being the first born, I had become accustomed to receiving a lot of attention. Lena and I would sit together in church on Sunday, she holding my hand in hers, and I twirling her diamond ring in the sunlight around her finger with the other. We were very close. Whenever she came for dinner, which was often, I would always sit near her. I would love to hear her stories of when she was young and the adventures she had. She would end her tales in a laugh and loved a good punch-line. Being in her nineties, yet in fairly good health for her age, I remember realizing the aging process for the first time and began to become painfully aware that one day I would lose my dear grandmother when God would take her to His home. Sure enough, that day came one sunny afternoon in May. It was 1973 and my sister and I and my two brothers had walked home from school for lunch. The minute I walked in the back door, I knew. It only took a quick glance at my father's face to understand the next words which were to follow his sad but tender look. He asked us to sit, then boldly said, "Your great-grandmother died today." That was pretty much it. I don't recall much being said after that other than none of us ate lunch that day, but went back to school to endure a grueling afternoon of sorrow.

You are never really prepared for someone passing. No matter how much we may understand the dying process, or have the luxury of preparation perhaps in one's death, the finality of death and the separation anxiety which follows is often times riveting. I teach in my spiritual counseling that you should not count on feeling a certain way, nor develop a preconceived notion of what you will undergo when the time comes you're told of a death of a loved one. Instead, be open to many possibilities of emotions that may arise. You'll in turn equal the playing field with the ability to cope and remove the guilt that often accompanies us when we react much differently than anticipated after receiving such news. It's healthier in the long run. Remember that there are no real grief guidelines, no right or wrong way, no magic number of weeks, months, or even years in measurement of the proper time to allow for the grieving process. Grieving is a natural and extremely personal experience which will be different for each individual.

The next few days around my house were spent preparing the funeral with very little conversation. Most of the focus was on my grandmother Claudia, since Lena was her mother. Assisting Claudia through this transition was a priority for my parents and grandfather. In those days you didn't talk much about death. You knew dead people went to heaven, and that was it. Enough said. End of story. We didn't understand post traumatic disorders and the like. Nor did we do well talking openly about our feelings. It was easier to sweep emotions under the rug and move on. We had been living in Lena's home in the city of Toledo, Ohio, while Lena had lived with her daughter Claudia and son-in-law Karl. Not long after Lena passed, we moved from the inner city, out to the country to a small northeast suburb of Toledo, called Oregon, and home to the world famous hot dog joint Tony Paco's, which Jamie Farr for all you M*A*S*H fans, made famous while he was on that TV series.

That first night in my new room was spent crying myself to sleep. I pleaded with Lena, praying to her and begging her to give me some kind of sign that she had come with me to our new home, and that she was indeed still around me. She had already been torn from my earthly existence, but now we had moved. Did she know where to find me? Would she know how to follow me to this new place? How would we still be connected? I can honestly say I don't recall ever getting a sign from her, although knowing what I know now, I'm confident she made the attempt. I was just too inexperienced or naive to witness it. I wouldn't hear from Lena again until 1999, while sitting in a Circle of Light (most of you know them as séances). Circle of Light sounds much more appealing and less grim don't you think? After all, this work I do is all about love and God's light, not dark, scary settings where tables and chairs are levitating.

In that Circle of Light I was practicing meditation with another medium in Dallas, John Cappello, who was leading the group of about twenty, in a room in the back of a metaphysical bookstore. After about an hour of receiving messages John said he had a female who wanted to say hello to me. Thrilled at the prospect that someone from the other side was working hard to make contact with me, I responded, "Great! Who is she?" John proceeded to tell me… "She says her name is Lena."

That same numbing feeling that I experienced years before when I heard the news of her death came over me again like a huge tidal wave. I sat there speechless and shocked that it was actually my beloved great-grandmother! Like a best friend who after years of separation decides to pop in to see you unexpectedly. You have had no time to prepare and have about a nano-second to say everything you've stored up for twenty some odd years. The math doesn't work. My mind racing, I could feel her love in the room with me and wrapping around me as if she was physically giving me hug. A warm sensation ran through me as I listened to John continue delivering Lena's message.

"She says she wished she could have stayed longer and that she was very happy with her life here on earth. She's holding her throat and saying that before she crossed, although she knew she was resting, she felt a slight tightness in her chest, and that it was becoming difficult to breathe. She is glad that she died while in her sleep and that her transition was very peaceful. She says that you were a beautiful baby Kathleen, and that she loved watching you grow."

I am still pretty much coma-like at this point and trying diligently to remember each piece of information John is relaying to me. He goes on… "She liked needlepoint and is showing me paisleys. She also likes vanilla. She says she used to put it on many pastries and desserts. She's leaving now but wants to thank you for giving her this opportunity to reach you."

Well, needless to say, I could barely concentrate for the rest of the session I was so overwhelmed with excitement. My husband was in the Circle with me and I couldn't wait to share my joy. I was on cloud nine! I had anticipated hearing from Lena for so long, yet she smartly waited until just the right time to make contact with me. You see, I had been working hard at perfecting my craft and concentrating on connecting with her for some time. Lena coming through for me that evening let me know that I was on the right track, and more importantly, that she was there with me once again, guiding me and assisting me when I needed her most. I was being rewarded.

As a highly developed medium, I can make that connection happen between a loved one and a client, however, as much as we would like, mediums don't have the ability to call upon our deceased relatives on demand. This isn't 1-800-DIAL-UP the Spirit World where we can just pick up an imaginary line and say "Can you hear me now...can you hear me now?" We do have the luxury of receiving messages from *our* loved ones when they deem it necessary. Even as I write this book tapping it out on my computer, while buried in this chapter, Lena told me that there was information I needed in a Bible which she gave me when I was eight. It's perched on the top of my credenza along with another one my uncle gave me. He found it on one of his hunts for Catholic treasure. My mother's brother, Bob is always sending me Roman Missiles, Rosaries, and Bibles. I have quite a collection now and am grateful to him for his kindness and thoughtfulness. Personally, I think he's thrilled that I finally married a Catholic and am raising my children in the Catholic faith instead of that 'fake religion' Lutheran, as he so affectionately refers to it. My personal belief is that there are many religions for many people...find the one that works for you. In studying near death experiences I determined that there seems to be one Maker, but that based on your religious beliefs, you will see either God, Jesus, Buddha, etc. You are responsible for creating your own relationship with your higher power. I choose to believe He's God.

I reached up, grasped the Bible, and then spun my chair around to lay it on the desk. As I pulled back the worn and tattered white leather cover and began to leaf through the pages I found my answer. Inside the second page was her inscription to me... "To dear Kathleen, from Grandma Moll, Christmas 1968." What was profoundly significant is what was written below her inscription.

Now keep in mind my ethnic background is a blend of German, Irish, and Scottish decent. In my research to grow my spiritual gifts later in life, the plethora of books I read by other mediums noted most had experienced at least one of their spiritual guides as being Native Indian. It began to strike me as a pattern and that if I didn't connect with an Indian in my quest to identify my guides…was I somehow lacking in ability? Did I not qualify as far as the spirit world was concerned to have one? In my many meditations I had indeed made contact with a number of my guides, yet they were never of Native Indian descent. I was not drawn to Shamanism either, although I respect the work Shamans perform. A dear friend and colleague of mine is a Shaman who teaches and performs numerous aspects of the Indian culture and traditions in rituals and dance.

Below my great-grandmother's inscription was, in blue ink, something I had scribbled back in eighth grade. As soon as my eyes fell upon these words, I knew exactly what this wise old woman was trying to show me. It said, *"Mamanowatum."* It is Cree Indian and translates to "Oh–Be-Joyful." A flood of memories came rushing back to me and discussions I had with this spirit guide. Of how I had requested my sister call me by that name because I felt such a strong connection to her. My sister laughed of course, and told me I was nuts and that she would do no such thing. I remembered going through a period where all I'd draw were pictures of Indians, animals, forests, trees. I even dressed like an Indian, although in those days the hippie look wasn't a far cry from Native Indian anyway. What Lena was letting me know was that I did in fact have an Indian guide when I was younger. I've learned through my experience as well as speaking with other mediums that our spirit guides change based on our needs at that particular time. We are continuously learning life lessons and although our guides are here to guide us and put people and places in our paths to help us along, we are entities of free will. They cannot and will not make decisions for us. We must grow spiritually from what we learn. So just as our needs and requirements of their assistance changes, so do they. We'll get into more specifics about the differences between spirit guides and guardian angels in Chapter 13.

As a young child, and then even as a teenager I would play mind games to keep myself occupied. Laying a spoon on the coffee table, I would stare at it forever, concentrating as hard as I could to make it move ever so slightly. Even if it budged a fraction of an inch, that's all I would need to feel vindicated that I really did possess magic powers! I just knew I did, I could feel it. Of course the spoon never moved, unless one of my brothers would sneak up behind me, blow on it, then hysterically run into the other room. When the phone rang I would try to guess who was on the other end before it was answered. Now *that*, I was pretty good at. Sensing people's emotions was another strong suit. "Déjà vu" tended to run hand in hand with my sensing abilities and was prevalent in my adolescent years.

My family did a fair amount of traveling as I grew up. My mom, born and raised in the Bronx, took us to New York several times to visit aunts, uncles, and cousins. She came from a large family so there were no shortages of relatives on her side of the family tree. I loved going to New York. I always felt at home there. I longed to live in a big city like that with the fast paced energy and great food and shopping. No surprise really that some years later I would marry a man from Brooklyn, and Italian at that!

On one trip to the Big Apple, I had gone for a walk with my uncle Bob while my mom and her mother spent some time together visiting. It was a beautiful spring day. We were sporting short sleeves and taking pleasure in the warm breeze as it caressed us on our stroll. Bob said he wanted to "stop by and see a friend since we were in that neck of the woods" and we would then head back to Grandma's. Sounded good to me. I was up for any adventure as long as it meant I was free to roam about and absorb the culture. We came to a large house on the corner and began walking up the steps of the front porch. As uncle Bob and I entered the brownstone, we crossed the threshold into a considerably large marble foyer. Standing in front of me was a vast circular staircase with a wooden banister. My eyes followed the flow of the swirling wood, up, up, and up. The farther up my gaze traveled, the more I sensed that I had been here before. This was all too familiar to me. I began to get a cold chill and quickly assessed that my presence at this place was not a good thing. An overpowering feeling of panic came over me and it must have shown on my face because my uncle took my hand and then asked me what was wrong. How do I go about telling him that I've been here before (as far as he's concerned this is the first time he or anyone else has ever brought me here) and that something so bad happened here that I just want to run out that glass door as fast as I can. Well a picture's worth a thousand words because without my uttering a sound, he simply marched me right out of there.

We didn't discuss it further on the way home. I think he just thought I was being shy or something and decided the visit to his friend wasn't worth the hassle of having a screaming kid on his hands. For the rest of the trip that staircase haunted me. I was uneasy with the feeling of urgency and despair looming over me. As if walking into that foyer made something attach its self to me somehow. I was confused as to what it all meant. I did know it felt reminiscent of bad vibrations of the past and a sensation I wanted to forget. At various emotional times in my life, that staircase would reappear in a dream or clairvoyant vision, rearing its ugly head.

As I was developing my gift and practicing a visualization exercise one day, I chose to try and work on the vision of the stairway and foyer, asking my guides for assistance in determining what had taken place there. They obliged. I was shown how a man had chased a woman to the top of those stairs where a physical confrontation took place between them. During the struggle, she toppled over the banister and fell to her death.

Whenever the memory of that incident now comes to mind, I no longer experience any feelings of dread, fright, and anxiousness associated with it. I typically only see it nowadays when my guides are using it symbolically to pass on a message or are trying to get me to say something related to it in a reading for a client. This was a lesson for me in karma, explaining to me how emotions attached to events become blockages in our growth. I believe there is a reason for everything we're shown. We'll talk more about karma, blockages and what it means later.

For as long as I can remember I knew I was different. Most children under the age of five are very open to their psychic gifts. A child's awareness has not been diminished by logical and rational thought patterns created by conforming to an adult society. Developing psychic skills teaches them to relax, to remain centered, to listen intently, and to see and understand what is around them in their world. These skills also show them positive ways of releasing emotions and puts importance on being in touch with their feelings and more importantly, their intuitions. They learn to become more independent and to count on themselves, rather than learn to manipulate adults into gratifying their wants and needs. We are all born with psychic senses and physical senses. Young children often see loved ones who have passed standing in the room right next to you! You can't see them but they can. Children haven't learned to turn this off, so they are using *all* of their sensibilities to soak in their environment. As a child I recognized that no one was interested in the fact that I could guess who was calling on the phone, or that I knew I had been in a place before somehow, even if my mother swore she had never taken me there. And sharing this information with friends went nowhere either. They were only interested in Barbie® and bicycles. So after a while, I just started keeping my escapades and games to myself.

Living in the country has its advantages. My parents own a nice piece of land sandwiched on a corner lot across a creek from a large state park. This made for fun times growing up, not to mention fulfilling my need to be in nature. It was beautiful. There were over thirty trees on their property, which included but were not limited to pear, apple, black cherry, and plum. Given that both parents worked, my mode of transportation if I were to get anywhere was my bike. I'd sometimes ride through the State Park and hang out by the massive duck pond and skip rocks. This was awesome meditation time for strengthening my gifts. The park was full of horseback trails and dense woods. Traveling to the park one day, I parked my bike against a tree and rested, meditating and praying.

After about 30 minutes or so my heart was so light and a beautiful sense of peace had come over me. I was enjoying feeling so connected to the exquisiteness of nature surrounding me, a oneness of me and the universe. It was truly a perfect day. As I stood up and climbed on my bike I began my trek home down a widened path which cut through the trees. The balmy wind began caressing my skin as I pedaled faster. I started to notice what I was truly experiencing. My senses were heightened and I knew an epiphany was about to take place. My feet stopped and relaxed on the pedals as I coasted in the warm sunlight. Gazing upward at the clouds I felt God's presence. I heard my named called out to me. Enthralled in an overwhelming sense that I was surrounded by my Maker, I knowingly felt him say to me, "You'll be taken care of….there is a plan for you."

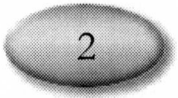

~ *Defining The Meanings* ~

Much of my life there seems to have been an anxiousness running through my veins. I could never quite shake it. This part of my personality would show in my various attempts to find a career path that would interest me for any great length of time. I married young in 1978, then divorced three years later. I would eventually meet the true love of my life while working for a computer company in the early nineties. Lou is an outspoken Italian (as if there are any other kind) who is caring, supportive and rates high on the compassion meter. He's an explorer like I am, not a follower, and we have thoroughly enjoyed one another now for well over a decade.

He had three children of his own from a previous marriage, and with my three that made six. When we married we knew we had our work cut out for us. Chris being the exception at five years old, the rest of the group ranged in ages from twelve to twenty-one. Since then, many years have passed and Lou and I reflect back to see a marvelous and tumultuous ride. We have beaten the odds and successfully built a remarkable family unit. We are truly blessed. Our children, LoriAnn 35, Stacy 33, Brock 27, Joe 26, Heather 26 and Chris now 19, have grown into wonderful, insightful and caring individuals, each different from the other, all making their own contributions which create what has now become a family of twenty-four (counting aunts, uncles, cousins and significant others in the family who have relocated to the Dallas area). We now have six grandchildren (including a set of triplets). We are together continuously enjoying dinners, games and family time.

Food is always a focal point of our get-togethers. Joe recently noted that after a large meal we all shared, he quietly counted to himself and then announced, "It took us only four minutes after the meal to start talking about food again!" Our family is not short on laughter or teasing one another either. Speaking frankly, nobody gets away with much without having to answer to someone in the group. Having the ability to laugh at ourselves, teasing is a regular past time. I rather like that quality we share between us. It keeps everyone in check with a great mutual respect for each other. The door to our home is a gyrating entry of constant activity. When we're together, everyone talks at the same time, the grandchildren are running under foot, and I just sit back and smile. I am rich beyond my dreams having been blessed with a home full of love and such a fantastic brood!

I have always been a working mom, and had tried my hand at several occupational disciplines in search of finding my 'niche.' Not to say that I didn't enjoy these jobs, I was just never really content or fulfilled. I worked for a staffing company, a large real estate firm, a computer leasing company and then eventually transitioned into an account executive job for a newspaper group in North Dallas. I grew a small sales territory, selling employment advertising, into a large and thriving account base which tripled my income in a five year period. I also conceptualized, created, and brought to market a bilingual employment newspaper. I was then asked to sit on their marketing board which governed eight newspapers at the time. I loved my job, but with all that, there was still a *knowing* that I was missing something. This just wasn't enough.

One of my duties happened to be inputting ad sales to meet the paper's deadline each Friday. This meant sitting at a computer for eight hours straight, typing. Now whenever your mind is focused on one activity for any great length of time, the subconscious will duly become bored and start working on its own. Most of us experience what I am describing as random thoughts that pop in our heads as we conduct our mundane task, whatever it might be.

When you study psychic phenomenon you come to understand that these thoughts are not always necessarily random and that the subconscious is actually stepping in front of the conscious. This is why meditation and visualization exercises are important in playing a key role in development. Training the mind to focus. Meditation is a purposely induced state where the physical body and conscious mind are bypassed temporarily so the inner self comes into focus. Sitting at my computer for such a long period of time and doing the same tasks over and over, created a map for my conscious mind to follow if you will, on auto pilot, and my subconscious started working very intently.

Around mid afternoon each Friday, I started experiencing what seemed like déjà vu. Only these were images of things that had happened in the past. It was as if a movie was playing in my head. I would suddenly see a memory flash in my brain of something which took place years earlier. Catching myself, I would stop and ponder, "Why that memory?" I'd shrug it off to being tired, over-worked, or just stressed and go back to business pecking on the keyboard. It wouldn't stop. Week after week I would endure these memory flashes. It became entertaining. I would chuckle to myself when Friday morning rolled around wondering which past events I would 'see' that day in my mind. At the time, I didn't realize there were larger forces at play. Not having an interest in the psychic realm, I had no clue that my spirit guides were working hard to get my attention. I was used to 'weird mind stuff' as I would call it, so I didn't really give it much thought.

After seven years at this organization I decided to do on my own what I was doing for my employer. I formed a consulting company that encompassed three divisions;

recruitment advertising, sales training, and career fairs for local employers in Dallas and Ft. Worth. The first few months went pretty smooth. We had a good infrastructure in place and were gaining momentum based on our individual client lists. Soon after though, things seemed to take a different direction. Although my business partner Becky and I had collectively, over twenty years of experience, we would take two steps forward, something would interfere, and we'd end up three steps back. From computer hardware problems to software glitches, you name it, the business started to become a calamity of errors. Regardless, we both committed to sticking it out for a year and forged ahead.

During this time, one evening while flipping channels on the television, my husband and I came across a new show called 'Crossing Over.' My husband shared my fascination with the host, John Edward's ability to seemingly communicate with the dead. We became hooked and started watching it frequently. I went to a local psychic fair with my daughter, Heather, and then found myself in bookstores reading volumes on the psychic realm and life in the hereafter. The material was captivating and I found myself mesmerized by what I was learning.

Things started to make sense to me. I learned to meditate and could, with much ease, put myself into a deep trance. I became skilled at recognizing that a quiet ringing in my ears was my spirit guides wanting me to listen or pay attention to something they were trying to show me. I started rekindling some of my old traits like guessing who was calling on the phone or who would be coming by to pay us a visit. Then things got a little weird. One night before drifting off to sleep I saw a vision of a car accident and then an ambulance rushing to the scene. Lou was still awake and I shared the vision with him. I told him I felt that my guides were warning me of this happening to someone close to us. Although I couldn't put my finger on who it was, I intuitively knew it to be a relative. The next day his daughter Lori would be involved in a terrible accident. She survived, but as a result, has had two back surgeries. After sharing what I saw with the rest of the family, I was mandated to always share anything like that should it occur again.

I went to Ohio that summer for my annual visit to see family, and while upstairs in my father's home office I was leafing through some books he had on a shelf. I found *Life After Life*, *Life In The Here After*, and several Edgar Cayce books. Surprised at the genre I discovered, I curiously asked my father what he thought of the psychic realm. He responded with calling it a 'spiritual' realm, and that he had been interested in Edgar Cayce's work for many years and owned quite a number of his books. He began reading about the afterlife when his step-father passed from a sudden stroke in 1979. I would later discover that this same grandfather would play a pivotal role in my life's work as a medium. I asked to borrow a few of his books. This was what I would consider my 'awakening' period. I became a woman on a mission. Reading a plethora of authors and subjects involving psychic phenomenon, I would attend 'Circles of Light' learning first hand about the process of communicating with the other side. I visited several mediums in my local area. My spirit guides seemed to be coming through rather well, but I was having difficulty reaching that place where I could hear from my loved ones who had passed. I wanted so desperately to make that happen. It was my largest motivator in exploring development of my psychic gifts.

One day I walked into a metaphysical store where a psychic fair was taking place. I glanced through the flyer which listed the bios of the psychics there. I was hoping my guides would steer me in the right direction. I decided on a medium I felt would be able to advise me on my obvious block in growth. He was a middle aged man, who appeared modest and unpretentious. As I sat down he immediately picked up on why I was there. He asked if I was looking for guidance in making that connection to the other side. I confirmed I was. I thought to myself, "So far things are looking pretty good. Think I chose the right one." As I explained my predicament, he gave me this advice, "You need to be open to hear, Kathleen. Your loved ones are trying to talk to you but you're too scared right now. You need to relax your mind and allow things to enter. You seek instant gratification and are expecting a different type of communication. When you meditate and visualize a garden, learn to feel it from in your heart instead of seeing it in your head."

At first I was unsure exactly what he meant by all that. I am a very pragmatic person, so that means I must see it, touch it, smell it to know it's real. The spiritual world is about seeing with a different set of eyes, hearing with different ears, and touching things with a different type of feeling mechanism. He told me not to get discouraged, but rather to keep working on my development. Concentrate on cleaning my mind. I worried too much about controlling everything. That in order for me to really 'hear' and really 'listen' I would have to first get rid of my old way of thinking. Not to force things to happen, but just let the opportunities present themselves. My guides would make sure that I saw them.

That advice made all the difference in the world to me. I was looking at this psychic development determined and focused and needed to see results before I would truly make a commitment to it. I was used to planning everything out in my life. Programmed after years of using finely tuned organizational skills and routines of the past, this was removing me from where I needed to be mentally, which was a clear and genuinely open mind. I took his advice and started focusing more on breath work and deep, deep meditation.

I made a commitment to meditate at the same time every day (which helps increase your success rate dramatically). Sitting in my bedroom meditating one afternoon, I was intensely focused, yet very relaxed. I was in the house alone when I distinctly heard my grandfather's voice say to me, "Get the slides." My grandfather has been dead since 1979. He was a deeply spiritual man, and had many times chosen to spend his Sunday afternoons sitting in the local jail reading the Bible to inmates. He could read the Lord's book in German as well as English. We were very close. He passed when my first son, Brock, was only a year old. Karl was an avid photographer and traveled the United States shooting pictures of landscapes. He developed the photos as slides for preservation. I received some of these slides after he died and have them stored neatly in a closet.

Scared, surprised and astonished all at the same time, I followed my instinct (and the voice), retrieved the slides, and came back to my bedroom with a bag full. Now if you know how slides are stored, they are usually kept in a long slender box, stacked vertically, each in their own individual slot. As I began searching through the bag which was full of many boxes, I asked my grandfather to show me which box it was I should be looking for. I heard nothing. I asked again, thinking surely if he went to all that trouble to make me hear him the first time, he would be compelled to answer me. I asked again. Still nothing. I began to doubt if what I thought I heard I actually heard. Or was it my just wanting something to happen so desperately that I manufactured it in my head? I remembered what the medium I had went to see told me, and kept looking.

I began removing box after box from the large sack hoping I would 'feel' which box it was he wanted me to view. Again I felt and heard nothing. I finally had all the boxes in front of me, strewn across the bed. Sighing in disappointment, I began putting the boxes back in the bag a few at a time. I was ready to give up. I had almost all of them back in the bag when as I lifted up the last two boxes, one of them dropped out of my hand and onto the floor right side up. The lid had flipped off and the box sat there, right side up. I smartly said to myself, "Okay, thanks Grandpa, I got my answer." I placed the rest and the bag aside. I took my handheld slide viewer and started to look at each slide in that box. As I placed each slide in the viewer, I kept seeing landscape after landscape. Nothing out of the ordinary jumped out at me. I was studying each picture intently hoping to see what it was Karl was having me look for. After about 10 minutes (I tend to be impatient) I asked out loud, "Grandpa, please show me what it is I should be looking for. I don't see any message if there is one, in any of the slides I've looked at!" I kept diligently looking and listening, and just two slides later, there it was!!!!

In the midst of this box full of landscapes; pictures of Yellowstone Park, the Rocky Mountains and such, here it was! A photo of a sole, red, heart-shaped vase of white and red carnations positioned expertly in the center of a small occasional table. The table had been placed in front of a hand made backdrop using a red quilted blanket. I was stunned! I now knew why my grandfather had worked so hard to communicate with me. He was sending a Valentine to my grandmother…you see, the date he was having me look through these slides was February 13th! I started crying and yelling out loud, "Oh my God! Oh my God!" I must have looked like a fool, dancing around my bedroom about to burst with excitement! Looking at the slide again once I had calmed down a bit, I now noticed there was a card inserted in to the top of the bouquet. The slide was so small the card wasn't legible. I quickly called Lou to tell him what happened and to meet me at the drugstore near our home. I had them blow up the slide to an 8x10. Lou and I, arm in arm, pulled the glossy paper out of the machine and gazed at it in silence. The card read, "To My Valentine, All My Love, Karl." I of course over-nighted the 8x10 picture to my grandmother. She was delighted. To get a Valentine from the 'other side' was quite a shock to her, but nonetheless very gratifying.

After that experience, while in meditation I would now routinely receive messages from both my guides and people close to me who were in the spirit realm. I especially could ascertain when either my grandfather or one of my guides, Charlie, was nearby. May had rolled around and the kids were anxiously awaiting the last days of school. One evening, late at night, I was having trouble falling asleep. It had been a grueling day emotionally. We had received news earlier that one of Chris' classmates, Baron, had died from an accidental death. My husband and I spent the day consoling Chris, trying to make sense of a senseless situation. I spoke with several mothers of children close to Baron and Chris as we shared ideas struggling to find the right words to comfort them. Finding it difficult to quiet my mind, I put on some soft music and started meditating, hoping that would put me into a relaxed state. I suddenly heard someone call out my name, "Kathleen." After repeating in my mind what I heard out loud, I recognized the voice…it was Baron. I could feel his presence there in the room the same way you sense when someone is coming up behind you. I didn't need to see him to know he was there. I asked him why he was here, and what else was it that he wanted to say? I received an answer but not audibly as before, this time it was intuitively. He said; "Just that I'm here. I'm okay." That was all he said and I felt his presence leave shortly thereafter. I was thankful and flattered that he would visit me. This would not be the last time we would speak. God and my spirit guides were working hard to show me that there was a whole other dimension that was very much a part of this one. I was becoming very thirsty for knowledge and an utter sponge soaking up any information my guides led me to. I knew there was a lot to learn.

Although extremely motivated to continue developing my gifts, I kept my day job despite the fact that Becky and I started joking at how maybe God just didn't want our business to flourish. We had all the right contacts, all the right connections, yet situations and circumstances kept being thrown our way that would delay our progress. We once had a company computer fixed twice by the manufacturer who told us they could find no legitimate reason why the unit was misbehaving the way it was. Our strong faith led us to believe that God had another purpose in mind for us and was steering us onto new paths. We kept at it however hoping He would give us a clear signal when it was time to throw in the towel. That next November another caveat would determine for me what I now believe is my life's purpose.

Several more months had passed and it was now the seventeenth of November. Our routine went undaunted, getting Chris off to school, and Lou retiring to his home office downstairs and mine upstairs. Just two weeks earlier we had taken my daughter and granddaughter to dinner. We had been gone only forty minutes when we returned home to see it raining inside the house. The water heater (which was in the attic) had broken just after we'd left, and had been continually pouring water first through the ceiling in my office and then the room below me, which was Lou's office. You are now starting to get the picture of what I mean when I say this company of mine wasn't meant to be. The flood wiped out my computer entirely (there was an air vent directly above it where pouring water, resembling a waterfall, destroyed the machine and hard drive), as well as most of my paper files. Lou's office was still pretty much in tact but there was a lot of water damage in the walls and crown molding, and the carpets were ruined. The insurance adjusters said we needed to strip all of the carpet upstairs and most of the downstairs out. We were walking around cement floors and still had the ringing in our ears from the eight mammoth industrial fans that had buzzed non stop for over two weeks, drying everything out.

You get to know someone pretty well after ten years together. When Lou yelled my name that morning and I heard it echo off the concrete floors, up the stairs and down the hall, I knew whatever he was calling me about was urgent. And not urgent in the way of, "Come here now!" It was more like, "Honey I need you now, something awful has happened!" I ran down the stairs and turned the corner in to his office. His face sullen and flushed, I knew whatever it was he was about to tell me I wasn't going to want to hear. "I have to tell you something, it's really bad, brace yourself," he began. I leaned against the wall for support and quietly said, "What…what's up?" I can hear the words thundering in my head now as if he is speaking them to me again as I write this. "Paul is dead," he said. "He was killed in an auto accident around three o'clock this morning."

I stared at Lou in disbelief and started shaking my head and saying "No" as if that would make it not so. Then with my hands over my mouth I slowly walked toward him. He grabbed me and we both cried for one of those eternal minutes. The ones where time ceases to exist. Suddenly he pulled me back, looked me straight in the eye and said, "We have to gather the kids."

Lou's ex-wife, Doreen, had married a kind and gentle man named Paul, the same year we were married. We attended each other's weddings and the four of us engaged in a warm and friendly relationship. Holidays, our children's birthdays and other events were often spent with all of us together. Doreen and Paul had moved to Henderson, Texas where they bought over twenty acres of rural land, just three hours outside of Dallas.

After building their dream home, Paul took a job driving for the mail service in that area and a neighboring town. The roads were slippery that evening of November 16th and Paul had been working a long shift. We are still not sure exactly who crossed the white line in the road, but Doreen, when watching the news the next morning, saw in horror an accident involving a mail truck and an eighteen wheeler. She knew that was Paul's route. Dazed and in shock she phoned her brother-in-law who lived nearby. Just receiving the news, he confirmed the report was true. Paul had been driving down a two lane highway at 3:00AM as a tractor trailer and he collided at top speed. The driver of the semi was catapulted through his front window, ending up underneath his own tires. Paul was killed instantly, his body mangled in the front of the small truck crushed by the eighteen wheeler.

We took in a deep breath and started the task of contacting each child. We asked that they meet at our home, and we would then head to Henderson together. One by one, they started arriving. As each child came, it was devastatingly painful as we tried to comfort them. Just keeping everyone calm and sane enough to make the three hour drive was challenging. We would have gladly paid big bucks to take a plane and be there in an hour if it were possible. From the time we heard the news until we left for Henderson, only about an hour had passed. We were now on the road.

When we finally got there, Doreen was excruciatingly numb. Each time she would come in to focus and be part of the room, she would scream at the agonizing and unbearable thought that her Paul was gone. For the most part that evening she would blindly stare into space, looking at us as if she was in some kind of dream and would wake up to find things back the way they were suppose to be. None of us had eaten and hadn't really even thought about food. No one wanted to cook but knew we would need our strength for the next day, so someone suggested we get some take-out and bring it back to the house. Lou and I volunteered and left for a nearby restaurant.

Henderson is a fairly small town and by this time it was nine o'clock at night. We ended up at a Denny's™. As we climbed into a booth and were about to place an order, my pager unexpectedly went off. I didn't have remote paging service so my pager should not have even been working in that area. On top of that, I had experienced problems with it lately where it would only work intermittently. Spirit once again was stepping in to make things happen. I read my sister's number in Ohio on the LCD screen. Puzzled I told Lou who it was, grabbed my cell phone and dialed. "Cynth," I said, "What's up? I can't believe your page went through. I'm in Henderson at Doreen's. My pager is not even supposed to be working near here. Why did you page me?" Not wanting to share the bad news with her yet, I figured I'd tell her after I found out why she was calling.

"I need you to go back to Dallas…tonight," Cynthia said. I now heard her voice trembling and was in disbelief that I was about to receive more bad news on this night. "Cynthia what's wrong!?" I demanded. "Mom is flying to Dallas…Aunt Anne suffered a heart attack this morning in Fort Worth. She's in a coma and has been declared brain dead. They are keeping her breathing until everyone can get there to say goodbye. She will be pronounced dead tomorrow. I've been calling you all day but not getting an answer. Finally I paged you."

Lou was puzzled, but from looking at my face, which must have resembled something out of Fright Night, he instinctively knew I was about to lose it. "What Kat, what the heck is going on?" He demanded. "Wait!" I said as I lifted my finger towards him to signal one minute. "Cynthia, I am in Henderson because Paul was killed this morning as well. He was hit by a Semi. It's real bad here. Doreen is hysterical and distraught!" There was silence on the other end of the phone line. After what seemed an eternity she said, "Oh no. Oh my God. Kathleen, Mom is coming." I returned with, "We'll figure it out. Lou and I will just have to go back and we'll deal with all of this somehow." Cynthia said good-bye after giving me the flight information and Lou and I then headed back to Doreen's to share the bad news.

Before leaving, Doreen took me through the house, room by room. The two of us walked in each room as she pointed to mementos and keepsakes that she and Paul had collected over the years. As we strolled into their bedroom I saw the large armoire Paul had refinished for her not long before. They had brought pictures of it to show us during a recent visit to Dallas and she had explained how he refinished it twice for her because she was unhappy with the color of the first stain he used. Paul was like that. He worshiped the ground she walked on, and in the five years they were together, had never (and I mean that in the literal sense) said an unkind word to her. He was a very gentle soul and a lover of humanity. Many people would come up to Doreen and the rest of the family over the course of the funeral to tell stories of how Paul had stopped to aid someone stuck on the side of the road, or of how he offered to repair someone's fence even when his own needed fixing. The stories came out of the woodwork. They say a man is defined by the people at his funeral. Paul was revered and admired by everyone who knew him.

Doreen was pulled away to a phone call received in the next room. I lingered behind and placed my hands on the armoire. I begged Paul to give me something I could pass to Doreen. "Give me some kind of sign to let her know you are okay. Tell me what to do to ease her pain," I said to him. I didn't really expect a clear and audible answer, but was hoping that over the next day or so maybe he would send something my way.

We drove back to Dallas around 1:00AM. When we finally went to bed, I collapsed from exhaustion. I truly don't remember walking up the stairs, let alone going to sleep. In the early morning as I was waking up I saw a vision. There were three plain looking cement steps leading to a screen door. As I stared and waited for what I would be shown next, the door opened from the inside. Much to my shock, there stood Paul! He was whole, in one piece, and appeared radiant as he smiled warmly at me, his red hair and wooly mustache shining brightly. Startled, the image then dissipated as quickly as it had come. As Lou awoke, I shared with him my vision so he would tell Doreen and the kids. I didn't realize it at the time, but looking back, I now know, they were not ready to experience my shocker of a vision. When emotional pain is so intense, doing simple functions like remembering where your keys are, is even complex.

I took off for Fort Worth early that morning, while Lou headed back to Henderson to help Doreen and the kids. So while I was attending to my cousins and mother with my aunt's death (I had two more uncles who flew in from New York and Ohio), Lou was assisting Doreen and the kids with Paul's funeral. To say the least, it was quite a nightmare. God gives you what you can handle, but sometimes the emotional upheaval is more than we think we can bear. Somehow He provides us with the resolve we require and we mull through, surprisingly stronger than we realize we are.

Anne was a diabetic. She had fought the disease for a good portion of her life. She was not in a high risk group though. Being under a doctor's constant care, her heart attack was sudden and not expected. In her mid 60's, she worked full time and made the most out life. Bingo was a passion of hers and quite often she would come home a winner, playing the numbers she also once won $65,000 on a Pick-Five lottery ticket. She shared the wealth and sent her children part of the money as well as her sister, my mother, Mary. After her husband, Earl passed a few years ago, she moved in with her son Tom. Anne and Tom were very close and enjoyed a great relationship. Both quite outspoken, they would take pleasure in debating just about any subject. The love they shared was incredibly strong, both anxious to defend the other should someone come between them. Anne had five children, Marty, Debbie, Catherine, John and Tom, being the youngest. Debbie lived in Tennessee and Marty, Catherine and John lived in Oklahoma.

As my mother and I drove to Fort Worth that day my mind was on auto pilot. When we arrived at Anne and Tom's I parked the car under the enormous oak tree that stood prominently at the end of the sidewalk, its branches dangling out into the street. Some of my cousins were mingling on the front lawn. We greeted them with hugs, kisses, and tears and proceeded inside. It all seemed so surreal. As if I was walking through a dream or a movie. I knew what was going on and who was around me, but felt outside myself somehow, as if a spectator just going through the motions. I walked passed a stranger standing by the front door and into the house searching for Tom. When I saw him we embraced and I could immediately feel his armor. An emotional protective covering. He was very direct and almost unemotional as he started to run down the game plan for the day. "We're heading to the hospital in a few minutes. The rest of the kids will meet us there," he said very matter of fact.

I looked at my mother and without words knew now who was in charge. As we turned to walk back out of the house, Tom opened the screen door for me and mom and I stepped through. Gazing at his arm pressed against the door of screen and aluminum I abruptly stopped. "Oh my!" I gasped. I stepped out onto the porch as I whipped around to get a good look at the front of the door. "Tom! I saw this door this morning in a vision!" I then turned to see three cement steps. Before, in my haste to speak to Tom I hadn't noticed the steps or door walking in. I had never visited this house before. Anne and Tom had recently moved into this house. "Tom, I saw all of this earlier today in a vision; the steps and that exact door, your Mom's angels are telling us she's not alone. I bet your Dad did this. He's letting you know he will be there for her when she crosses over," I said, overjoyed. Tom on the other hand smiled courteously at me, but remained focused and purposeful in his actions. "Come on Kat, we need to go," he said. I just looked at mom and smiled. She understood what I was talking about and was comforted that Earl had let us know Anne would be okay in her journey to the other side.

The funerals were scheduled on different days and I was able to attend both. Although we have a large family, so many of Anne's friends came that they filled half of the mortuary and had made large buttons for each member of our family. They walked around the funeral home searching for family members and pinning them on us. We were all so touched by such a kind and thoughtful gesture. Each button had #34 written on it, her employee number at Kmart where she worked. The design of an angel holding up a heart made of roses was at the top, with an inscription at the bottom which read, "In memory of Anne Reed." She was an avid collector of bells for years and possessed well over a couple hundred. Tom set up a table in front of the podium next to the casket with an arrangement of a few of her favorites. He delivered an eloquent eulogy and her grandson Michael, who was eighteen at the time, spoke as well. The day was somber yet at the same time uplifting, seeing the many hearts that Anne had touched and the lives in which she had made a difference.

Paul's funeral however was somewhat different. There were two services, one in Henderson where he passed, and one in Dallas where he was buried. The service in Henderson was the same day as Anne's funeral so Lou attended there while I went to Anne's. Although Paul had been held together with gauze and bandages under his clothes, Doreen wanted an open casket. She was depressed and despondent and the kids were doing their best to hold her together. A day later the burial service for Paul in Dallas was gut-wrenching. When Italians mourn, they tend to be very vocal. Releasing emotions at the time of the hurt, rather than storing the anguish for later seemed to me to make more sense anyway. Lou and I drove behind the white limo carrying Doreen and the children in the slow procession making our way through the cemetery. As we pulled in front of the gravesite and parked, Doreen stepped out of the limo screaming. Approaching her without the ability to make her pain disappear, we could only watch as she stammered to the casket and threw her arms over the metal casing crying and weeping saying over and over, "My Paulie's dead! My Paulie's gone!"

We left the cemetery that day knowing things would never be the same for us. Doreen, my husband, I and our six children had a piece of our lives ripped from our being without our consent. I would watch over time as each of us would go through the many stages of grief and bereavement; anger, frustration, denial, and the immense sense of loss. How do you resume your life? So much had changed. Each birthday and holiday event would be forever different with empty chairs to remind us of the loved ones now gone. I found myself asking again and again, "Why did things have to change? Why couldn't we go back to the way things were?" I came to the aching realization that things were not going to be the same. It was up to me to adjust and create an amended life for myself and my family. We would rebuild!

I thought about the many families that suffer the loss of a loved one. It's inevitable for each of us. I decided then and there, one month after the deaths of Anne and Paul, where my energies would be directed. Becky and I folded our company two weeks later, a year and a half after opening its doors.

I used my new found spirituality to not only overcome the trauma of the losses we suffered that November, but to also dedicate my life to assisting others in grief and bereavement. I committed my life to helping others develop the spiritual gifts and psychic abilities God has given each of us. Life is eternal. There is a great healing process and knowledge gained in receiving messages from Spirit. Making that connection to your loved one on the other side is simpler than you think. I hope that in reading the following chapters, you will come to understand what I did; that life is eternal and never ends. Our Maker has a great plan for each one of us. It is up to us to dig in to the resources He provides us, and use them to their fullest potential, so we might learn what He desires us to know; we are all part of Him. That loving ourselves and each other is all that really matters. Through Him and in Him, with love all things are possible.

~ *Simple Symbols, Huge Validations* ~

When I first started taking appointments as a psychic, I would read tarot cards. I could communicate with my spirit guides, and feel the presences of my loved ones when they were around, but was not confident yet if my guides felt I was ready to channel spirit for clients. I was content to pass messages to them using the cards, providing guidance and instruction regarding their future. My ultimate goal was to channel for others creating that connection for them between the physical and spiritual worlds. I continued to work on my skills as a medium and joined various circles.

Word of mouth quickly spread that I was an accurate reader and I soon built up a fairly good clientele. I found often, as I would read the tarot for my clients, I would get bits and pieces of information regarding their loved ones passed. It might be a first name, or that they just had a birthday, but my communication with souls in spirit was still unsteady. I went to see a good friend of mine, a fine medium who had practiced the art of communicating with spirit for over twenty years. I asked her what she thought I might be doing wrong. Was there a blockage of some sort that I wasn't aware of? If I wanted this so bad, why was I not able to make it happen, yet I could be extremely on target when reading cards for someone? She told me that there were two sides to my development. An emotional side having to do with my heart's desire and a spiritual side having to do with my mind. "My mind and my heart were not working as one," she said. I needed to let go of my ego self, stop trying to control the process and let my guides and spirit have power over the practice of communication.

She was right. I prayed for guidance in allowing my controlling side to quiet, while I raised my vibrations to reach the spirit guides and loved ones of my clients. It worked! I began getting messages like crazy each time I would do a tarot reading for someone. Ultimately it would turn from a card reading session into a reading of speaking with spirit. I was now asking my guides if they felt I was ready to only channel spirit in a reading for a client rather than do tarot.

I had contacted an organization in Dallas which hosts a large psychic fair each month at a local hotel to get on their list of readers. At the time they said they already had enough readers, but would keep me on their contact list should an opening arise. Two days after I asked my guides to give me sign that I was ready to set the tarot aside, I got a call from Rita and Barbara, the organizers of the Dallas psychic fair, asking me to participate. "What kind of a reader are you?" They asked. "Do you read the tarot, or are you a clairvoyant?" I decided to seize the opportunity I felt my guides were giving me and said, "Actually neither. I'm a psychic medium. I talk to dead people." "Is that right?" Barbara said, "Hmm...I don't believe we have anyone that strictly speaks with the deceased. We have checked out the references you gave us and would be pleased if you would join us next Sunday at the fair." I responded with, "I'll be there."

As we discussed the particulars I was nervous. Reminding myself that my guides had not let me down yet, I heard them tell me this whole psychic thing is based on trust. Trusting the information you receive from them, and trusting that spirit knows better than you most of the time, what is best for you. So I continued to follow their lead and walked into my first psychic fair where I would be giving readings connecting with spirit.

The response was enormous...I was booked the entire day! I read for twenty-two people that Sunday with no breaks. I was utterly exhausted and energized all at the same time. Once again, my guides proved to do just what they are supposed to do, guide me in the right direction. The rest is history. Over the past several years I have learned a great deal with regards to the profound power of spirit and the influence of our Maker in our daily lives. I am repeatedly gaining knowledge of the afterlife and how our two worlds blend on many different levels.

Speaking to spirit for a living has its advantages. Besides the joy of getting to experience so many interesting and intriguing family stories from my clients, there is also the added dynamic of the healing that can take place when definitive validations come through for loved ones left here in the physical world who are grieving. (Especially when it involves someone in spirit answering a direct question asked by their loved one while in a session.)

A woman by the name of Rene was referred to me by another client. I was told that she would be calling me and that she just wanted to 'check out things that may be coming up for her in the future.' It was on a Wednesday, just a week prior to Thanksgiving that she visited my office. By communicating with her spirit guides and mine, we began discussing what was going on in her life at the moment and what she could expect in the coming months. After about thirty minutes into the session, Rene told me she knew I also contacted people in spirit and although open to whoever might come through, indicated that she would like to try to connect with her mother. I told her I couldn't promise who would come through, but that I would try my best to contact her mom. What follows is a brief account of the rest of my session with Rene. Pay close attention to the end of our meeting and how her mother gives Rene proof that she was aware of the circumstances which took place immediately after her physical death.

"I smell apples Rene. Does that mean anything to you? Are apples an important reference for you or your mother?"

"Yes...that's my favorite dessert my mom used to make me. It was an apple strudel thing. My mom and I always had this telepathy thing going on when we were on our way to visit each other. I would always wish/tell mom in my mind that I wanted that apple thing and she would always have it made for me."

"Your mom is showing me the month of April. She's saying that is an important month, someone's birthday or anniversary."

"Yes, that is Ryan's birthday, my son."

"She's saying that someone in the family is a nurse or works in a clinical or medicinal setting of some kind."

"Lana, my brother's wife, her sister Pam is a nurse."

"Your mom is now showing me a name starting with the letter J. She is wanting to make reference to someone connected to you who has a name that starts with J."

"That could be Johnny her deceased brother or Jared, my nephew."

"Your mom is showing me tulips. I am not getting anything else other than she is just fanning tulips for me. Does that hold any meaning for you?"

At the time Rene couldn't think of anything, but when she got home that evening, there was a birthday card for her husband Rodger's mother sitting on a built in desk in her kitchen area that had tulips on the front of it. That was Rene's mom's way of indicating that she is around and can see what is going on in their lives.

"Your mom is telling me that she passed in March...is that correct?"

"Yes."

"She is also telling me that your dad fell on a shovel or a tool of some sort. I'm seeing this outside somewhere, like in his yard."

"Dad has fallen so many times and on tree stumps and at the tool shed. I really don't know if he actually fell on a tool or not. But I know he has fallen several times and works with tools a lot."

"Your mom is describing the small step porch which is at the back of their house she says, correct?"

Now that we've been flowing for a while and the session is picking up momentum, so is Rene's energy level. With much enthusiasm and sitting up in her chair, she leans forward over the desk between us and eagerly answers.

"Yes, that's correct."

"Did your mom read the Bible? Not all the time she's saying, but occasionally. She is very spiritual."

"Oh yes."

"Just so you know, she understands exactly what it is that she wants to convey here. She wants me to tell you again, she says, that she was ready to go. Did you know that?"

"Yes...mom told me many times that she was ready to go."

There is a long pause and once again, as if regaining the energy needed to go on, Rene's mother starts tossing out detail after detail of events which took place while she was here, as well as occurrences after she passed.

"Rene, your mom was a big dancer wasn't she? She's showing off for me, twirling around, smiling and joyfully prancing to music."

"Oh yes! She absolutely loved to dance!"

"Your mom wore glasses right? She's showing me that she has glasses on."

"Yes, she wore glasses."

"And she had short curly hair, yes?"

"Yes, she did!"

Excited that her mom was showing herself to me, Rene's voice heightened as we went on.

"Before she became ill, she said she very much cared about the way she looked. She is describing herself as meticulous and tailored. That she had to have everything matching, just so, purse, shoes, clothes, etc."

"Oooooh yes...she definitely always looked nice."

"You recently put up a fence didn't you. Mom is saying she watched you construct the new fence."

Rene giggled at this and just shook her head back and forth as if in disbelief as to the accuracy and accounts her mom was throwing out of things which had taken place since her passing.

"Yes, we sure did! The fence is for our dogs. My husband Rodger did an excellent job. It's a privacy fence on one side of the house."

"Mom is saying that someone just celebrated a birthday! She's wishing happy birthday to someone connected to you."

"My brother just did in October, a few weeks ago."

"Mom is showing me that she had red lips. Did she wear a lot of red lipstick?"

"Yes, she always wore red lipstick. It went with her reddish hair."

"Mom is saying now that she has one of her sisters with her in spirit."

"True, mom has two sisters that have crossed over."

"Rene, she is now pointing at her throat. She's saying there was a breathing problem or difficulty breathing. Your mom passes because of a breathing problem. She wants you to know that she is okay now. That she no longer has this affliction and is very comfortable and happy where she is. She's aware that she passed because of that and that it was okay. It was her time to go."

Rene nodded her head solemnly and responded.

"Yes, my mom was on a 100% oxygen breathing tube for several years before she passed."

I paused for a moment as I waited for more messages to come through.

"Mom throughout the reading today, keeps showing me pumpkins. When I ask her what she wants me to say about them, she's not really coming forth with any particular answer, she just makes them bigger in size, as if the emphasis is on the pumpkins themselves. Does that mean anything to you? Were you or mom known for baking pumpkin pies?"

"Mom baked pies, but I had actually baked this pumpkin thing once that mom really liked."

"She's doing it again. Given that Thanksgiving is around the corner, could that be it?"

We both laughed at the timeliness of her message and coincidence of the holiday. Rene, spoke eagerly and with passion.

"That's what it is! We all loved thanksgiving so much because it was the one time during the year the family would all get together and bake and eat all day long. That was our time of family togetherness. Christmas's were spent with Rodger's family and Thanksgiving was with my mom and dad."

"Your mom is talking about a head injury and that something was wrong with her eyes. She's saying she had trouble with bifocals and that her lenses were different in each eye, correct?"

Smiling, Rene goes on to explain why her mother is making reference to this.

"Yes! When my mom was much younger, she fell and hit her head really bad which messed up one of her eyes. She could move it inwards, but when she tried to look outward, that one eye would just stare straight ahead."

"She's now saying your dad does wood working."

Throwing herself back in the chair Rene exclaims...

"Wow! That freaks me out! Yes!"

"Mom is really taking her time and being methodical about what she's showing me in detail what dad did with the wood. She's showing me he's cutting lots of pieces and then fitting them together very carefully."

"My dad does what's called 'Intarsia.' It is where you have many pieces of wood that you put together to make one big picture. Kind of like a puzzle, but where each piece is made out of raised wood. Even different types of wood. They are very beautiful and unique pictures."

"Mom is saying that she kept a journal of some sort. She's showing me her writing things down, recording things."

"Yes...she kept a little book of all the times she took her medicines and what medicines she was taking. She had several of those little notebooks lying around that she had filled up. Plus she was always writing down the weather, the day and time she saw the weather, etc., and she would always write little notes on pieces of paper."

There is another long pause. I'm now hearing a foreign language. I engage Rene to assist me in deciphering what it is her mother is trying to tell us.

"Mom is speaking to me in Japanese. Did she speak the language or ever take a trip to Japan? What is this that she is trying to convey? Do you know?"

Rene responded... "No she didn't speak the language, but she had Japanese figurines and pictures everywhere all over her house."

We both laughed at the technique Rene's mom used to get that message to us and I jokingly offered that mom might have been of Japanese decent in a previous life. Rene agreed, saying that she and her brother kidded their mother about that because she was always drawn to Japanese stuff and they could never understand why!

"Your mom Rene has a very sweet, warm personality. She's showing me that she had many friends."

"Indeed, yes...everyone loved mom."

At the end of a session, I will always ask my clients if there is anything they would like to ask the spirit. I tell them while I cannot guarantee they will answer their questions, more often than not, their loved one will undoubtedly give my client a response to their question that is both detailed and validates the information queried. What happened next in the session surprised even me. And I have witnessed some pretty amazing and hair raising phenomena in my line of work. I knew from Rene's body language and responses, that she was happy with our session and that she believed this really was her mom she was communicating with. However, what was to follow I found, was the enormous power held in one small validating sentence that would change Rene's life forever.

Rene stated that she and her brother Steven were with their mom when she passed. Because of the nature of her passing and Rene's mom being somewhat incoherent at the time of her physical death, Rene wanted to know if she realized that they were present when she died. I responded to Rene.

"Oh yes, she knew...but let me ask her if she can verify this by giving you some specific facts or details surrounding her death."

I no sooner got those words out of my mouth, when I saw a vision of her mom lying down on a gurney, someone attempting to cover her with a white sheet, and Rene screaming "No!" She showed me Rene was pleading with someone not to cover her mom's face. Although I am diligent about relaying all the information I receive from a spirit, this was a tender and emotional situation, and I didn't want to get it wrong in the translation. I proceeded gingerly hoping that what Rene's mom was showing me was the message I was to deliver.

"Rene…was there something different about the way she was covered? *Or to be more precise, was there an issue with covering her after she passed?*"

Rene started to weep and after gaining her composure, softly said, "Yes...when the funeral home came to get my mom after she had passed, I asked the guys to please not cover her head until they took her out of the house. I pleaded with them saying please....do not cover up her face, I just can't stand it. So they didn't until they left the house!"

Now at this point I felt Rene's mom was beginning to step back and the session would be over soon. I discovered quickly, her mom had other plans. She had plenty more that she wanted to say.

"Rene…who is it that grows tomatoes? She's telling me she wants to make reference to the person who grows tomatoes."

"We do, my husband Rodger and I. We put a lot of effort into it."

"Well that is just your mom's way of letting you know she sees what you are doing and that she is still near you."

Given that her mom was receptive and informative the last time she asked her a question, Rene considered giving it another shot and asked if her mom would validate for her that the vivid dreams she experienced where her mom would speak to her, was in fact 'visits' or just ordinary dreams.

I told Rene I'll ask and see if her mom will verify anything. If these really are visits from her, then she will tell us something detailed about the dreams or what it is she said in the dream, so you'll know that it was indeed a visit. There was a small pause and then her mom was very clear and deliberate with her answer.

"She's saying there was a large body of water in one of your dreams."

"Yes! One of the dreams was that mom was in our house and we were talking in the TV room and the lake is my backyard! I really believe mom is visiting me when she talks to me."

"Your mom is saying Rene that she loves being on the other side. She loves the freedom of no responsibility and she is at peace there. She is very happy. What she loves the most is that she can be in one spot one second and then instantaneously, she can be somewhere else. Do you write letters to your mom since she's crossed?"

"No."

"Your mom is showing me that you communicate with her in some way."

"I talk to her every night after my prayers."

"Oh, I see. That's her way of letting you know that she hears you."

"Your mom was a very visual, very descriptive person when she told a story correct? She's saying that she was a little flamboyant in that way."

"Oh yes."

"Your mom has decided it's time to leave now. She is walking to a door, opening it, and is actually turning around and waving good bye. She's quite a colorful character."

"Thank you so very much for this. You have made me very happy. I know that mom is with me at all times and that makes each day a little easier for me since she crossed over. She was and still is so precious to me. I wish she could have talked with you when she was alive. She loved spiritual stuff. She had several readings; eye analysis, life regressions, etc. She has a ton of books on the subject at the house too. I think I will get them and start going through them."

Rene left my office that day on cloud nine. I was clearly amazed by her mother's ability to be articulate when communicating the messages she wished Rene to have. From the thousands of readings I've done, I've come to know that most often a spirit will hold on to their personality they had in the physical realm. Their demeanor and the methods which they use to process information is very much the same on the other side. If they were eloquent and expressive while on the earthly plane, they will communicate in much the same manner from beyond. If they had a difficult time communicating with others while here, they in turn will have a harder time developing an understandably clear symbol language by which they can convey their messages from the spiritual realm. There are of course exceptions to the rule. I have seen spirits come through many times in readings very clear, when their loved one I'm reading for states they wished their loved one would have spoke that much and that clearly when they were here on earth. That's the thing about being a free will entity. We have choices. Earth is a learning ground or school if you will. With each one of us plodding through our chosen lessons. Some of us learn fast and for others it's a more graduated conquest. The old saying is true…it's all about the journey getting there, not the destination.

In my psychic development classes, I teach my students that there is a great responsibility attached to doing psychic work. Especially when reading for others, never censor anything that you receive from someone in spirit. What may mean absolutely nothing to you, will be a huge validation for the person you are reading for. I have learned through experience to never discount any piece of information I'm given. Even if it makes no sense to me at all, it always, inadvertently has a meaning for them. It is not up to you to decide which information gets passed on, and which doesn't. You will find that if you censor, you will be inaccurate in your ability to relay the messages properly so they make sense. Spirits have a huge advantage over us in the physical realm. They have the ability to see into the future, and they can understand the dynamics that are at play with everyone connected to the person being read. They will access that knowledge and use every helpful piece of information possible to expend the least amount of energy to get their point across. They are into bargain shopping for words and symbols. It takes an extraordinary amount of energy on their part and they will be selective in what they say and how they say it.

For instance, I had a mother and sister in my office one day for a reading. They had several relatives from the other side who came through with messages during our session. Although it was what I would consider a quality reading, I could see in their faces disappointment in not connecting with someone, and we were almost to the end of our appointment time. I asked them who it was that they wanted to hear from that we had not yet connected with, telling them to only give me the nature of the relationship of the person to them, and not their name. This is what followed…

"Kathleen, we were really hoping to connect with my brother" the daughter responded. "We know a medium can't just call up whoever we want to speak with, but we would love to hear from him if there is any way."

"Let me see what I can do." There was a long pause as I tried to see if I could make a connection.

"I do have a male around you Bobby," addressing this to the mother. "I believe he's saying the name Russ or Rusty. Does that have meaning for you?"

Both ladies smiled vehemently, "Yes, yes that's him. We called him Rusty," Bobby's daughter Judy said.

"He was in the military? He's showing me a military uniform."

"Oooooh Yes." Judy started answering all my questions at this point.

"Hmmmm" I said and paused for a moment. Perplexed by what was showing me, I asked him to clarify and then began again. "Rusty is showing me a file cabinet. I will try to be as clear as I can on this so you understand exactly what it is he's showing me. It may not mean a lot to me but I have a feeling you'll be able to understand what it's about. When I ask him to be clearer he just shows me the same thing again, so here goes."

The two women now leaned forward and intently listened. They had gone from exuberance to absorbedly serious in a matter of seconds.

"Okay, Rusty is showing me this filing cabinet right? But he says this cabinet has to do with his death. There is a lot of mystery surrounding his passing he's saying."

"Yes that's true, go on."

"He says it's very clandestine, that there is a cover up of some sort. You two were not given all the details, do you know that?"

"Damn straight. We knew there was more to his death than we were told!" Bobby and Judy grab each others hands.

"Well I think he is about to unfold it for us…hang on" I said putting my hands up as if to slow down what was being said. "He is being clear in saying that he did not pass the way the doctors said he did. He died in a hospital right?"

"Yes that's right" Judy said.

"Well he is showing me blood. Did he have a problem with his blood? That's the way I'm getting it from him."

"Yeah, sort of, let's see what else he says."

"Rusty is showing me that the blood is how he dies. They gave him the wrong medicine in his blood he says!" As soon as those words came out of my mouth, both women jumped up and back down on their chairs.

"Yes! That's it! We knew it!" they screamed. "Now it makes sense. We knew this is what happened."

"Again he's reiterating though that the doctors covered this up so how would you know? He's saying the doctors didn't admit that they had made a mistake. He says the records are sealed and that you cannot get to them, correct?"

"Yes he's right. You're right in all of what you said. But the reason we know how he died is because of what happened the night before!"

"What do you mean" I asked captivated by what Rusty had just told me.

"The previous night before he died, we had gone to visit him in the hospital. When we arrived, he told us that the doctor on call had tried to administer to him a blood thinning drug that should have been given to the man in the bed next to him. Rusty was a hemophiliac. Hemophilia means your blood doesn't clot like it should on its own. Complications such as bleeding into your joints are common for hemophiliacs. A blood thinner given to a hemophiliac is as good as a death warrant. Fortunately he awoke as the doctor was about to put the needle in his arm. When Rusty requested to know what they were giving him, he and the doctor discovered the mix-up. As the doctor looked at Rusty's chart at the end of his bed, he apologized to him and then gave the medicine to the right patient. He was fine that day when we saw him and they expected him to go home very soon! The next day when we went back to visit him again, is when they told us he had died that evening. When we asked why and what was the cause of death, they said it was classified. We knew something wasn't right. And we knew we were not getting the whole story!"

"I am so sorry" I said as I shook my head in sadness. "I know the military can sometimes quickly close ranks in a situation involving one of their own. I can tell you that Rusty is now saying though that it doesn't matter. He has forgiven them and he just wanted to put your minds at ease. Rusty is saying that you now have your suspicions confirmed so you can let it go. He's saying you want to sue the government?"

"Yes, so we can see the medical records. But our attorney is advising us that we would be fighting an uphill battle and that more than likely we wouldn't get anywhere anyway."

"Well if it's any consolation, Rusty is agreeing with him. He says it won't change anything. To just let it go."

"Is he okay now?" Bobby asked softly.

"Yes, very. He is a strong presence and is showing me his arm muscles like Popeye you know?" I responded laughing. He's literally flexing up one arm and making his muscle pop out."

"That sounds just like something Rusty would do" Judy chimed in.

We ended that day very introspective, all three of us. I love my job as a medium from the perspective that every spirit and every family I come in contact with has their own unique stories. Some sad, some joyful, but none the less, intriguing. Each session I hold is a learning opportunity of what's important to our loved ones in spirit, why is it they choose to make contact with us, and what motivates them on the other side. Bobby and Judy were lucky enough to be steered in a direction where their fears were put to rest and they could attain some closure surrounding the death of Rusty. I was just glad I could be a part of that process.

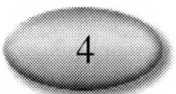

~ *Why They Don't Quit* ~

As a medium, I get messages randomly. We are not immune to spirits knocking at our psychic doors now and again when we're not asking for it. Although we train to turn it on and off at will, spirits can be very persuasive and will go to just about any length to get their messages heard. If we are not seeing their signs and symbols, they will resort to other methods to get our attention. Remember in chapter two my son's young friend Baron who passed? By this time Baron had come to me several times and was always so pleasant and gentle in his method.

I began teaching psychic development classes. It was a warm spring evening and I was just wrapping up a training session with a student. When Tonya and I first met there was an immediate sense of warmth and compassion and we were quickly becoming close friends. I had done two readings for her and knew she possessed the ability to be a good reader herself. She only needed someone to connect the dots for her. After participating in one of my development workshops she was going to practice channeling. We did this in my office to make use of the good energy there. I had requested she try psychometry (the art of reading vibrations off of an object) and channel for me in that way. I encouraged her to just trust the information she was about to receive and that everything would go fine, trying to calm her fears. Holding my wedding ring she nervously began. After a few minutes of silence Tonya said;

"Kathleen this is going to sound weird but I am getting the feeling of a cruise. I think it's a cruise ship of some kind. Or you are on a cruise."

I am accustomed to symbolism and it has become a second language for me so as soon as Tonya said cruise I immediately thought of the last cruise I was on. I began to smile wryly and said, "Go on."

"I'm getting the feeling that this cruise is not planned, that it happens suddenly. That's weird, that can't be right. Why would you go on a cruise at the drop of a hat?"

"Tonya, what you're saying makes perfect sense to me, please go on. You are right on the money."

"You're kidding! Okay. Well I think this is a male coming through and he's now giving me the feeling of a carnival, and a festive feeling, balloons, you know, stuff like that. He's saying the word carnival."

"Wow! I can't believe this is happening. Tonya this is so awesome, go on."

Apprehensive, Tonya laughed and continued, "Okay he is showing me a banner now. A very large banner and it's hanging real high in the air."

At this point I am about to lose it. Keep in mind that one, I am usually the sender not the receiver, and two, Tonya's ability for accuracy was uncanny given this was her very first time channeling.

"Tonya he is being very detailed about what he is giving you. Continue, but remember to tell me everything you are being shown and told."

"Okay no problem, Kathleen. I am. He's now showing me a patio...there's an umbrella on this patio like what you would see over a table and chairs."

"Yes...I know what he is referring to. What else is he showing you?"

"The patio and then a beach...this patio is on a beach somewhere."

"Exactly" I exclaimed with much enthusiasm. Tonya is getting keyed up too and is talking at a faster pace now.

"There's a stretch of beach, blue water, and those grass huts you see in travel brochures."

"Yes…Yes! What else?"

"There are two people walking in the sand. They have flippers on…and goggles, you know, snorkeling gear."

"Wow…Tonya this is wonderful. What you are describing is so perfectly accurate as to what I experienced. This spirit is taking you down memory lane. I know what he is doing. I'll tell you after we finish. What else does he have to say?"

"Well as long as you understand what it is he's saying that's fine by me, because I don't have a clue as to what all this means! He's singing a song now. It goes… 'On the hills of the harvest moon.' He's showing me a big golden moon now. "

"Hmm…I'm not sure what that means but go on, maybe he will clarify it for us."

"He's saying what sounds like the names Larry, Stanley, and now Steve. I'm not sure it's hard to hear it."

"That's okay just keep going."

"Ooh, now he said Matt. I heard that very distinctly. Matt."

"Oh my, that is his father's name."

"Now he's saying Micky D's. I guess he means McDonalds? I'm not sure."

"That's okay; we can always check it out later with someone else who knew him. Maybe he loved McDonalds" I said grinning.

"Now he's showing me a salamander. I'm not sure what he means by that either. I'm just seeing the lizard."

"Okay…I don't recognize that as well, but keep going. Let's see what else he has to say."

"Kathleen…" Tonya pauses and looks at me fixedly as if she doesn't want to say the next item.

"What?"

"He is letting me know how he crossed. He's showing me he's choking. He says that choking is what led to his passing."

I nodded my head slowly, "Yes, it is."

He is smiling now and is showing me his face. He had a round face didn't he? And thick blond hair, and a really wide smile," Tonya smiles big also as she conveys the message. "He has lots of pearly teeth when he smiles."

"Yes…yes he does. He had a beautiful smile."

"He says it's time to go now."

"Okay…thank you for coming Baron."

"His name is Baron?"

"Yes…Baron."

Baron's passing was a great shock to everyone. My son, Chris, who was twelve at the time had never experienced the death of anyone close to him, relative or friend. Baron's mother was one of Chris' teachers, and Baron's death was extremely personal to him. He had known Baron since the first grade and had shared many classes with him throughout elementary school. Then while in Jr. High, they shared a class called 'Industrial Tech' which Rose, Baron's mother, taught. This passing was new territory for us as parents and we were a little unsure as to the best course of action in consoling Chris. We knew we should be direct and truthful about everything with him, but we also were aware that his friends, and his other teachers, colleagues of Rose, were all affected by this. The entire school was in mourning.

Baron passed in May. We decided that when Chris finished school in a few weeks, we would take him on a cruise. Getting away, just the three of us, would provide the opportunity to spend quality time with Chris and put the focus on healing what we were experiencing. This was the sudden cruise that Tonya (or I should say Baron) was referred to. In fact it was the Carnival cruise line we were on, which is why Baron gave her a carnival feeling. The balloons and banner which hung very high, is in a picture we took of Chris standing on the top deck leaning against the railing on which a large banner hung with the Carnival logo. We were on the lower deck looking up at him on the top of the ship when we snapped the picture. While docked in the Bahamas, we disembarked to walk around Nassau one day and while on the island, stopped in at the Marriott hotel. We cut through the hotel to play on their beach for a few hours. We had parked our gear and towels underneath one of the blue umbrellas perched over the tables on their patio. Sitting around the table, again we had someone take our picture. Lou decided to read, and Chris and I stepped onto the beach in our snorkel gear to test the water. We walked the entire length of the Marriot beach that day in our flippers going in and out of the water looking for seashells. When we stopped to rest, we were under a grass hut, one of many which were sprinkled on the beachfront providing shade for tourists. There was a *full moon* that trip and we had admired it while on the Lido deck at night relaxing in lawn chairs. I'm unsure of the names Larry and Steve, but Baron had mentioned his father's name also, Matt. There *was* a salamander on the beach that day also at the hotel and I now remembered we had seen many walking in Nassau. Tonya had described Baron perfectly. He was a very jolly child with thick blond hair, a round face and toothy grin. Recounting what led to his passing was right on as well. Baron knew that by telling the nature of his passing, it would leave no doubt from whom Tonya was receiving her messages.

Tonya informed me she felt another presence coming through. This time it was a female. I sat and waited for a moment, when she began again.

"This woman says that she crossed suddenly. She's showing me she's feeling very tired and then is slumped over the steering wheel in a car. I'm getting the feeling that she didn't get to go home. She didn't get to where she was going. She says it was early morning when this happened."

"That's exactly right. I understand Tonya. I recognize this. Go on," I said grinning.

"Okay, well she's showing me a lantern, like she's carrying it to see in the dark. I'm getting Tulsa, as in Tulsa, Oklahoma."

"Really! That's great, yes, what else?"

"She's saying the name Mary. Is her name Mary?"

"No that's the name of her sister. They were very close."

Tonya nodded in acknowledgement. "Now she's showing me she got hit in the head with a board! Do you understand this?"

"No, but that's okay, I know someone who probably will. What else is she saying?"

Tonya paused for a moment and then began, "Hmm, she is showing me a wishing well, you know the kind with the small roof over the top and the bucket and everything. She's giving me the feeling you would throw pennies in there to make a wish."

"I'm not sure what she means, but I'll write this all down so I can ask her son later."

"As you said that Kathleen, she said the name Tom. Who's Tom?"

"Whoa…that's her son."

"Okay now she's showing me a Toto looking dog, like the one in *Wizard of Oz*."

I smiled, nodding, "She describing one of her dogs to you."

"She says there is a picnic being planned. She is showing me what she looked like. She had dominant cheeks and short hair. She says she always wore it short. She's saying another name now...Linda or Lindsey...I think it sounds more like Lindsey."

"Oh my Tonya, you two are really connecting. She just gave you the name of her first grandchild!"

"She's showing me what Lindsey looks like, blonde hair, ponytail and she wore it braided too she says."

"Wait until I tell her son, Tom, all of this. He will be so shocked."

"She's getting weak Kathleen, I can't really get anything else from her."

"Tonya, thank you so much. This will mean a lot to her son Tom, they lived together when she passed and I know he will be glad she came through." With that, we ended the reading.

After the session Tonya and I discussed what it all meant and the many validations that had taken place. I had been meaning to call my cousin Tom who lives in Fort Worth for some time. Both our schedules are busy and months had passed since I had talked to him. Up until then, the last time we spoke was on September 11, 2001. We have a lot of family that work in New York City. We suffered only one loss that day, on my husband's side, his cousin's sister-in-law. We feel fortunate in the fact that it wasn't worse. My Uncle has a hardware store near 47th street in Manhattan and he spent that evening assisting people when and where he could. One of Lou's other cousins Linda, worked on the 39th floor of one of the towers and had already survived the 1997 bombing of the World Trade Center. Probably what saved her life this time. When the first plane hit that September 11th, she knew immediately something was very wrong. The entire building shook. It was chaos with some people shouting out orders to stay put, others yelling to go to the stairs. Screaming that her co-worker was in the bathroom, she wouldn't leave until she saw her. As her friend finally exited the restroom and they turned for the stairs, the bathroom literally exploded. Racing down the stairway and blinded by smoke, heat, and ash, she stretched her arms out in front of her and found the shoulder of a stranger. He grabbed her hand and led them down to street level. Police and firemen threw them into a building next door as they yelled at them to shut the doors tight. They no sooner entered when her tower came crumbling down. Linda watched as thick black smoke funneled in under the doorway. Then everything went black and it was as if they were in the depths of midnight. After a short time, she exited the structure and running through the madness, made her way on foot to one of the ferry's taking the ride to safety to Staten Island. Linda would later get a transfer to a branch of her company out in Jersey and swore she would never work in the city again.

We were all profoundly changed that fateful day and I will forever be humbled by the many heroes who emerged in time of adversity in New York as well as those in the rest of our country and throughout the world.

I immediately called my cousin Tom after Tonya left. I had been feeling Anne's presence around me the few days before Tonya's reading and felt her urging me to check on Tom. I had procrastinated and she made her point. I was slacking and not calling Tom as often as I should. It was my responsibility to not drop the ball. When we spoke and I shared with him Tonya's reading, he was very receptive and thankful for the messages from his mother. He explained some of the references that I hadn't understood. The wishing well Tonya had seen was actually the name of a store that he frequented. Tom's an avid collector of wizards, dragons and other mystical creatures. You can find those in the Wishing Well and his mother had purchased things for him from that store. Anne had lived in Tulsa for many years and that was where she had raised Tom. The board thing Tom explained was a story Anne had told him which happened long ago when she was a young girl. A boyfriend of her mother's, Johnny, had once hit her in the back of the head with a two by four and had knocked her out cold.

I visited Tom's home that next weekend and did another reading for him. Anne came through loud and clear. She named the restaurant where he and his partner Jimmy liked to have breakfast, spoke of a camping trip they were planning, and many other validations. Although I find it difficult to give readings for family members and rarely do it, I was glad to have been the bridge between Tom and his mother. I know it gave him some closure and a sense that his mother was still watching over him. Something he really needed. Tom had been left with the responsibility of making the decision to take his mother off of life support. According to her will, she gave Tom the ability to decide if heroic measures were to be taken in the event something drastic took place.

Anne was taking her dogs to the vet the morning of her death. She was leaving the vet's office, had loaded the dogs back in the car after their appointment and was behind the wheel with the car still in park when she had an apparent heart attack. The women in the office watched as they saw Anne suddenly grab her chest and slump over the wheel. By the time the paramedics arrived and could administer CPR, she was already in a coma state. Once hospitalized, it was determined that Anne was brain dead and that life support would only prolong the inevitable. The rest of her children and family flew in from around the country. Paying our last respects, the Priest held a service in her room and then Tom did what he had to do. He shared with me months later that he was very angry at having to make that decision. He had consulted with his brothers and sisters on what to do and the doctors had proven to him that Anne would not improve over time, but it is a tremendous task to feel that even remotely you have the balance of another's life in your hands. Tom felt, he said, "As if he had carried the weight of that decision for everyone else in the family." They were not the ones signing the release for removing the equipment that allowed their mother to breathe. That's what he was frustrated over. Carrying that burden. It felt unfair to him. The rest of them could feel comfortably removed from that part of the process. Over time Tom has realized though what it meant to his mother, and more importantly what *he* meant to her, because she had given him that responsibility. Anne showed him the fearless and undaunted trust she had in his judgment. That she felt completely at ease with her life in his hands. That her deep love and commitment to Tom was never ending, no matter what the outcome.

Separation anxiety, in my opinion, is the most crucial and most difficult components of losing a loved one. The notion of never speaking to this person again, holding them and touching them, leaves a deep void that no words can fill, now matter how well intended they might be. In psychology there is an idea factor called the dual-process method. This method entails creating a spiritual relationship in place of the physical relationship you once had with that deceased. It assists the healing process specifically in dealing with the 'void' issue. I have worked with counselors where they assist patients in the various stages of the grieving process and I step in, in the latter part of their treatment to help create development of that spiritual relationship with their loved one. Through learning tools and specific instruction individuals in grief grow to understand how to recognize signs and symbols from their loved ones, as well as fundamentals for maintaining a 'new' spiritual relationship with them. I do suggest to anyone reading this that if you are in the beginning stages of grief, please seek some type of counseling if you are having a difficult time coming to terms with your loss. We all suffer emotionally when a loss occurs, however we each have our own individual thresholds for pain and grief. Do not let anyone; friend, relative or counselor, tell you that there is an allotted time for your grief. There is now magical hour when you will suddenly pass through an epiphany and will no longer grieve. Just as we are all unique, so are we in the grieving process. There is no right or wrong time or place to grieve. There are no restrictions on how to grieve. Bereavement is a very personal experience and should be treated as such. Society has for many years set the bar it seems at one year. That one year is a sufficient amount of time for a person to go through the entire grieving process. I've spoken to many people who are of the opinion that in one year's time, their loved one should be able to get on with their life. What they might fail to see or understand is that the first year in bereavement is usually spent trying to attend to financial details, possibly selling a home or relocating, figuring out how to 'fit in' when your family unit has been reduced by one, etc. The bereaved seldom have time to grieve properly in that first year. Also, the family of the person grieving is traditionally very supportive and there to assist in aiding them through the many particulars they must endure that first year. Moving into the second year, the rest of the family is now taking *their* time to grieve and trying to get on with *their* life, inadvertently leaving the bereaved individual to fend for themselves and in some cases, feeling abandoned. There are so many components to each situation so there are no clear cut answers, but if we understand that each person grieves differently and on their own time schedule, we will be better equipped to administer the proper support and understanding needed.

In learning to develop a spiritual relationship with your loved one, the ultimate message from them is that they are still near. They see into our lives and are there supporting us even if it is from beyond our own physical dimension. Just 'knowing' that they are okay and around is what most of us require to feel comforted and strong in moving forward. Baron and Anne were not about to give up until I passed along the messages to those who so desperately needed to hear them.

~ *Strength In Numbers* ~

We all know that when in the presence of a large group or say while attending a seminar, most of you will experience a shift in your adrenaline flow. Your vibrations are actually rising and you are operating a different speed than normal. We can sense or 'feel' the excitement in the air as we prepare to listen to the speaker. It is true, at least for me, that there is a significant change in the way spirits operate to get their messages across when in a group atmosphere. Many dynamics are at play and there is a long list of reasons why a group reading will differ from a private one. For the moment let's focus on the positives. There is power in numbers, we all know that. Why, is because the combination of energy patterns in one common area dramatically increases with the number of life force it contains. Imagine the size of the light generated by one 60 watt bulb. Now compare that to the light generated by fifty, 60 watt bulbs.

When I conduct group readings, there is a tremendous amount of life force at work, all interconnecting to produce a desired outcome to bring about the readings and messages for those who are supposed to receive them. Spirits understand that by working collectively, they can deliver more messages, than by working alone. These opportunities they know are rare and when they get a vehicle as easy as a medium ready and willing to be a messenger, they will work hard to get the most value out of the energy being used in the room.

A good example of this is taken from a group reading I did in Dallas at a local hotel. This is a partial account of the readings which took place that day. I've tried to include the specific parts of the session I found to be interesting which will show you the exceptional patterns which spirits use. There were approximately sixty individuals in attendance. The event was held in a theatre rather than a ballroom because I liked the stadium seating. I felt everyone would be more comfortable and I would have a better view of my audience. As people were entering the theatre and I was backstage meditating and getting ready, spirit was already knocking at my psychic door. I could tell they were very excited about tonight's event and one spirit in particular was going to make sure that he was heard. He told me his name was Charles and that he would be hanging around until I was able to connect with his loved ones in the audience. This isn't uncommon. Any good psychic medium will tell you that no matter how controlled our abilities may be, we sometimes meet up with spirits who are enormously determined and have a mind of their own. They are the ones who tend to be very creative in their messages and will go to great lengths to be recognized. I told Charles I would do my best, and asked him to please guide me as best he could to his loved ones waiting.

After I was introduced, I briefly ran through how I get my symbols and messages to the audience members and then began the readings. I announced to the room that I had a Charles who had visited me backstage and would anyone like to claim the name Charles. A woman raised her hand and I proceeded to walk towards her to try and zero in on her energy. As I approached her Charles gave me the month of March. I asked her, "Is there a March connection for your Charles?" She looked back at me with a sigh and shook her head, "No." I waited to see what Charles would say next.

Another woman raised her hand as I said, "This Charles is showing me a garage. He is claiming to have taken his own life. He is saying that the garage is strongly connected to him in some way. I think he's trying to say that's where he committed suicide." I was headed to the other side of the room now and half way there when a second woman said, "I know someone who took his life in a garage but his name isn't Charles."

I soon became aware of what was happening. "He's now showing me that he used the car to end his life is that right?" "Yes that's right," she responded. I went on to give her other validations from this spirit coming through for her, but knew that I had 'switched' and that Charles had politely stepped aside to let the other spirit has his five minutes of fame. Soon I was on the move again and asked if there was a Cindy that was connected to travel in some way that anyone could claim. Again four people this time threw their hands up into the air. "Uh oh" I thought to myself. With the momentum now generated in the room I was hoping I wasn't being faced with relative stealers and that the spirits would cooperate in getting me to the right person. One by one, I read each individual with their hands raised and briefly gave them more information pertaining to their respective Cindy's; each of them receiving validations ranging from pet names to birthday dates to anniversaries. All except one, none of the people with their hands up could acknowledge a minister connected to them in their circle of family and friends. It was a very strong symbol. I explained to the audience that their relatives were working together on the other side so messages being given would fit several people at once.

All the while, I could still feel Charles' presence yet he was remaining remarkably quiet. I was shown this minister again only larger and told that that too was some how connected to a Cindy and that there was an educational component around it as well. This time I felt Charles literally push the other spirits out of the way as if to say, "Okay it's my turn now." I felt an immediate pull to the left side of the room and quickly made my way in that direction.

"I am going to do something out of character here," I told the room. "I typically don't do this because I do not feel it's fair to single someone out and have them ask a question. Not everyone here tonight will get a reading, but a spirit is now being very definitive and is leading me to you."

I pointed to a mother, and what appeared to be her daughter, sitting a few rows back. "I hate to put you on the spot like this," I said, directing my finger now at the daughter, "But this spirit I know is for you, his name is Charles, and he says I must ask you to do something for him." The young woman began to shake and nervously nodded her head indicating that she recognized a Charles in spirit. Her mom laid a hand gently on her arm to give her some moral support.

"By the way, just so you know this is the same spirit that visited me backstage. He's been trying to connect with you all night. He says that there is a specific question you want to ask him. What is it?" I quietly waited for her answer.

As she drew in a deep breath she said, "I just want to know if he's okay," and began weeping.

"He is very okay. He says he is your brother correct?" Now the messages came like rapid fire. "He is showing me a garage again. He's placing a lot of importance there. And he is saying that someone just graduated or finished school." I see the mom nodding her head and pointing to herself. Addressing her now I asked, "You had taken Nyquil® to sleep at night after his passing is that right? Charles is saying that you had trouble sleeping after his death and that no one realized you took this Nyquil® to help you sleep!" Leslie (the mom) was floored. There was a look of shock on both our faces.

Leslie responded with: "Yes, oh my gosh, I cannot believe he said that! No one knew!"

I said smiling, "Charles knew!" Everyone in the room laughed. It was a nice ice breaker and the tension in the room seemed to ease a bit. I quickly kept going, trying to keep pace with the images Charles was showing me. "He's apologizing for taking his own life and says that no one could have helped him here. He knows that you feel there is something you should or could have done to prevent this, but he's clear in saying that nothing anyone could have done would've changed the outcome. He knows that he didn't show any signs of depression. That no one knew he was as down as he was. He is sorry for hurting you. He's saying there was a chemical involved. There was a chemical in the autopsy report."

Both women were nodding their heads in agreement. Intently listening, they waited as Charles continued on. "He is bringing up the designer, Tommy Hilfiger. He's showing my Tommy Hilfiger clothes."

Leslie said, "He loved Tommy Hilfiger! That is all he would wear. We buried him in his favorite Tommy outfit."

"He's stepping back now, but he is glad that he was able to speak with you and he wants you to know he is still around you."

With that we concluded the readings and Leslie later filled me in on what some of Charles' messages had meant. Leslie's boyfriend at the time was an ordained minister. Charles was making mention of the minister so she would know he recognized her relationship. Leslie is a High School Guidance Counselor and had just concluded her doctoral study course work. Again Charles was letting her know he was around and was proud that she had finished it despite the emotional upheaval she was experiencing at the loss of her son. The garage connection for Charles was that it was his private domain. He was always in the garage practically living in there. He had set up a workshop and would be in there most of his waking hours. The drug found in the autopsy was dopamine. Charles was born with a chemical imbalance and a diagnosed schizophrenic. His Aunt Cindy is a travel Agent and Cindy had recently lost her own father right after Charles' suicide! Charles was born and died in the month of March.

What this group reading showed me is that several people received important validations and messages from their loved ones. But the messages were received in such a way that the spirits were obviously working together on the other side and therefore increased the number of individuals who were 'read.' Had they not worked together, I would have had a lesser amount of people I connected with that day for sure. I do not believe in coincidences and I do believe that God placed all of those people there that day for healing. Even those who did not receive personal messages walked away with a true awareness. An understanding that the power of spirit is real, that our love for each other is what maintains that connection between us and our loved ones, and that we will each get our own personal signs and symbols from those in spirit.

Another way I've found spirits reach those of us on the earthly plane is taking advantage of massed energy in small groups. A good friend of mine, Marco, shares in my line of work. He had popped over for lunch one day and as we were visiting he started getting messages for my mother-in-law, Helen. As it turned out, her father, Biagio, had come through to let her know that he knew she had relocated from Brooklyn and had moved to Texas. She had inherited the home from her father. It was a two family dwelling with her, her husband and two children occupying the upstairs, and her brother, sister-in-law, and their children occupying the downstairs. This type of multi family dwelling is common in Brooklyn and had turned into quite a piece of real estate. It was very difficult for Helen to make the decision to leave her home of forty-two years, but after much consideration, she decided to be closer to her family and made the move down south. Nervous about whether she had made the right decision, it was clear that it put her mind at ease to know her father was happy she had made the transition. Marco told her that Biagio was also aware of her financial gain from the sale of the house and to enjoy the money. That she had worked hard all her life and deserved to have it. After several more messages Marco ended and Helen thanked him. This wasn't the first time that Marco had brought Helen's family through and it was getting to be a common thought of who Marco might bring with him whenever he visited. My mother-in-law of course always looks forward to his visits as well as I.

Not long after that visit, Helen, my daughter Heather, and I were gathered around my kitchen table. We had a tarot deck, and I was teaching my daughter some specific card spreads. As the three of us were chatting, my cell phone started ringing. I picked the phone up from off the table and glanced down at the display screen to see who was calling. Not recognizing the number I asked Heather if it was one of her friends maybe trying to reach her and passed the phone to her. She opened it and said, "Hello." No one seemed to be on the other line. She said hello several times and was about to put the phone down when it started ringing again. She had not touched any of the keys on the phone. With her eyebrows cocked, she handed me the phone. All three of us were puzzled as I took it from her hands. As I held the phone to my ear and listened to it ringing another phone, things got really strange! All of sudden Helen's phone starts ringing. Her cell phone had been lying on the table also. We all look down at her phone to see my cell number on her display screen! Helen picks up her phone and shuts it off. I turn my phone off and then back on. The three of us sit there in silence. Our phone numbers were not programmed into each other's phones. That means that even if (for you skeptics) Heather did accidentally push a button, which she didn't because I was watching her the whole time, my phone couldn't have dialed Helen's. As we sat there baffled and a little weirded out, my phone rings again! We all jumped. Then laughed at how stunned we were. I looked down to see the same number who had originally dialed me the first time. This time I answered. "Hello," I said cautiously.

"Hey Kat, it's me Marco."

"Marco! Did you just call here a minute ago?"

"Yeah I did, but no one answered."

"Oh someone answered all right, but I think Biagio is having fun with us."

"What do you mean?"

"When you called a minute ago, Heather answered the phone. She said hello three times yet no one was on the other line. Then my phone started ringing on its own and dialed Helen's phone!"

"What!? You're kidding."

Laughing I said, "No, I'm not kidding. I think Biagio used you to reach out to Helen. You are the common denominator here. Since he seems to like using you to get messages to Helen, I think he just took advantage of your energy and connection to her and sent her a little hello. It's the only thing that makes sense to me."

Strange occurrences, or what most people might consider strange, happen around our household quite bit. We have since gotten used to the spiritual inhabitants and with the exception of a couple of our children, the rest of us pretty much take things in stride. Lights can go on and off by themselves, we've found pieces of tissue floating in not one bathroom toilet, but all of them at the same time repeatedly, and it's common to hear footsteps in our hallways at night. I can usually pick up on which one of my loved ones it is that's visiting us at the time. I welcome signs and encourage them to get creative. I once came home to find several picture frames arranged on an occasional table in my den, lying face down. I was the first to arrive home. The children at the time were in school, and Lou had not yet arrived home from work. There were no windows left open and we owned no pets. I just smiled to myself and placed the pictures back in their upright positions. It never happened again. But then, why would it? They made themselves known.

My husband's grandmother died before he was born. His mother Helen was just fourteen years old when her mother passed. Lou's grandfather remarried before Lou was born and subsequently, he only knew one grandmother. That was until now. When I started seriously working on fine tuning my psychic skills, Lou would frequently tag along. He found elements of the metaphysical world intriguing so he didn't complain too much. We were participating in a circle of light one evening when the medium in charge addressed Lou. "I have an Ann coming through Lou. She says she is strongly connected to you." Lou did that thing all mediums dread and shook his head. "I don't know an Ann in spirit," he said. "Are you sure, Lou? She says she has been around you all of your life. She has watched you grow since birth. This isn't a spirit guide I'm speaking to Lou. This is someone who once inhabited a physical body," the medium said. He continued, "She is a large woman and is very strong in spirit. This was a strong willed woman when she was here." Lou still couldn't make the connection and the medium said the spirit at that point pulled back her energy. We left that night a little perplexed but figured maybe we would be shown at a later date who this was and that she would appear again in another reading.

Almost a year later we were visiting his mother in Brooklyn, helping her to prepare for her move south to Texas, when Helen got out a box of old papers from a bureau in a back room. As she rustled through the papers she lifted out of the box an old mass card in remarkably great shape. As she handed the piece of paper to Lou she said, "Hey, here is your grandmother Ann's mass card." We both looked at each other and it felt as if we were in slow motion. I watched his face as he took the card and read it. He looked up at me speechless at first. After fighting back a few tears he said, "Mom, she came to me." Helen then said, "What do you mean?" Lou responded with, "Grandma appeared in a Circle of Light Kat and I attended last year and kept telling the medium that she knew me since birth. That she is always around me watching over me. I never really knew her so I didn't recognize the name Ann when he said it to me. This is who it was. It was grandma!"

My mother-in-law showed us pictures of Ann and she was a large stocky woman. Helen described her as very strong willed and never at loss for words. She said she was a very take charge person. Just as John had said she was. Since that incident at my mother-in-law's, Ann has come through several times now in various readings. It's as if once we acknowledged her, she now is a frequent visitor. She is funny at times, very stern at others. She once came through to scold us for not putting her picture in a frame and out with the other family photos. Lou had received a copy of the picture from his sister after the whole mass card thing. The picture, you could tell, was obviously taken in a studio and had that brown sepia look. Ann is sitting on a chair with her hands folded in her lap with her hair pulled back in a tight style. She is poised with her head tilted upward and has a striking presence. After he had received the picture, Lou originally shoved it into a pile of papers where it had sat on his desk for several months. After her scolding, it was in a frame and in the den with the others by the next day.

We learn what we know to believe as truths of the spirit world from encounters such as these. My experience has shown me that the more you are in and around the environment that is conducive to communicating with spirit, the more you learn from the various things said and done in these sessions. I have grown to understand more about what I feel takes place in the spiritual world, before and after we cross, from my conversations and lessons of those in the beyond, than I have in the culmination of all the books I've read. I do encourage anyone interested in learning more about the spirit world to read. And read a variety of authors and topics involving the spiritual mechanics of the afterlife. But go to spiritual circles also. Attend group readings where you will witness the many forms of spirit coming through. It is a huge learning process and a wonderful landscape on which to absorb the many symbols and styles of communication used both by different mediums, *and* the spirits themselves.

My grandmother passed in 2002. Lou's grandmother and mine of course had never met in this lifetime. When you are a psychic medium, who are some of your friends? Other psychic mediums, naturally. Edgar is a high spirited, generous fellow who always has something kind to say about everyone. We were in my office one day discussing work stuff when he said, "I have someone wanting to come through to you." This is not uncommon when I sit and pow wow with my psychic friends, so I said, "Okay…who is it?" Edgar responded; "She is a large woman with very dark hair pulled back tight, like behind her head. She's holding her head up very high. Her chin is pointing slightly upward, proud like."

"I know who you're referring to, go on."

"She says she's not talked about very much. And she's claiming ethnicity. She showing me she's not Anglo-American."

I chuckled. "No she is very Italian! And she's right. We don't speak of her much because she was gone before we were born. She's not usually in the family stories we tell."

"Well she's saying she wants to be talked about more Kathleen. She doesn't want people to forget her. She's also saying she had experienced pain in her lower rib cage section."

I just shook my head and smiled. "That sounds like something she would say, based on what her daughter has told me. The lower rib cage is from the gall bladder disease." I wasn't prepared however for what happened next.

"There is another woman with her Kathleen. She's claiming she has an older woman who is there next to her who wants to say 'hello'."

I wrinkled my brow not sure of whom Edgar would be referring to. Patiently I waited to see what he would say next.

"She says a stroke was the cause of her passing and that she died just recently. I'm getting a grandmother feeling. She has white hair and says that she loves the color purple."

My heart started racing as I came to the realization of who Ann had next to her. My grandmother who passed only a month before had been buried in a purple suit. It was her favorite color and she was an amazing seamstress. Claudia had went shopping, picked out the pattern and material and then sewn that outfit years before her death specifically for her burial! Needless to say she was a little particular about how she looked. Always impeccably dressed, she was going to make sure she looked marvelous on her last day her loved ones would see her.

This was the second time that my grandmother had appeared in a reading (the first is in the next chapter) and It's my belief that in each reading spirits try to provide us with information of what's going on over there and how things work. Our grandmothers were teaching Lou and I that even though they didn't know each other in this lifetime, connected by the bonds of love between Lou and myself, they were now hanging out together on the other side. Cool! I slammed my hands down on the desk in enthusiasm and nearly scared Edgar to death. We both laughed and I shared with him what was happening. We both agreed that two heads were better than one and that they had figured out on some level, by working together they could achieve more than working alone. This wouldn't be the only time they would appear together in a reading. So far as to this day, they have come through collectively three times. This tells me that our loved ones that we knew in this lifetime are there to greet us when we cross over, but it also means to me, that who we are connected to here on earth will also determine who we meet once in spirit. Pretty awesome, wouldn't you agree?

~ *Validating Their Power and Presence* ~

While standing in my kitchen one morning at 10:00AM my cell phone broke the silence by playing the jingle which alerts me that a new voicemail has arrived. Not hearing any ringing prior, I thought it strange that it would go straight to voicemail. Walking over to check it out, the LCD screen on my phone read "1 NEW VOICEMAIL." Curious, I hit the call button which normally allows me to see what phone number the voicemail was generated from. There was nothing to view on the screen, just the option to retrieve the message. I dialed voicemail and began to listen in shock as I heard the following message. "Message sent Thursday, December 26th at 3:50PM.....Hi Kathleen, this is Tracy. You may not remember me. I had a phone reading from you I think back near the very end of September or the first week of October. I have family here from another country visiting. I know this is last minute but I thought it would be a good idea to try to arrange a conference call phone reading with you. I wanted to see if you would have any time available. If you get a chance please give me a call back at your convenience."

What makes this so strange is this message originally came in on the 26[th,] but it was four days later, the 30th! This was the same voicemail I had already saved and placed in the 'saved box' on my cell phone and then called Tracy back on the 26th and did a successful conference call for her and her stepfather that day. You will read about the conference call in chapter 8. Laughing, I smiled and walked into the next room to explain to my husband what had happened. Since these types of occurrences are very common around here, my better half has created his own buzz words to describe them and thereby cut to the chase when referring to anomalies in our life. When I told him of the message, he just rolled his eyes, chuckled and said, "The *spooks* are at it again, eh?" I dialed Tracy and left her a reciprocal voicemail to let her know that her mom was trying hard to get my attention and obviously had a message for her, and to please call when convenient. This was our exchange when Tracy called me back.

"Tracy! Hi, thanks for returning my call. Do you believe this?"

Tracy is laughing but somewhat nervous.

"I know. I just can't believe this. This is weird huh?"

"Well, yes and no. I have had spirits use the cell phone before to get my attention. This isn't the first time. I believe that different mediums get different types of communication from spirits based on whatever is the best way to reach them. Some mediums experience visits from loved ones of their clients who are crossed over in their dreams, etc. You know? They (spirits) have the ability to turn on electronic devices like radios, TV's and stuff at will. The cell phone is no different. For whatever reason, they've chosen to use cell phones with me."

We both laughed.

"Since your mom was successful in doing this, whatever it is that she wants to say must be very important so I'd like to read for you okay? Is now a good time?"

"Absolutely, I really appreciate you doing this."

"No problem...I'm as curious as you are to see what she has to say. Okay, give me a second here to get things rolling."

There is a long pause of about a minute or so.

"Okay, Tracy someone is coming through, do you know someone name Rita?"

"No, I can't think of anyone named Rita off hand."

"Now she's saying Patricia. Do you know a Patricia?

"Yes."

"She's showing me putting on what looks like riding boots. These black riding boots are connected to Patricia in some way. That's the feeling I'm getting from this. This is definitely mom coming through, I know her presence. Are you attending a circus or event that is like a circus atmosphere soon? That's the feeling I'm getting."

"No not that I can think of."

"Wait…she's saying that this event is like a small gathering of some kind. Not a big blow out party but just a few people getting together. She says this is happening relatively soon. Do you know what she's talking about? Are you doing something like this soon?"

"Not that I can think of…wait, there is a small get-together happening at work coming up."

"She's putting casual around it. This isn't a formal meeting right? It's a more casual setting or meeting."

"Yes that's right."

"She's now saying the word bubbly, making reference to champagne. Are you doing something special for New Years, a small get-together of some kind?"

"No we are just staying home. I wasn't planning on going out, unless something changes and this comes to pass."

Tracy giggles.

"She's saying you take the train to work. Do you have to take a train to get to work?"

"No not normally, but I will be taking a train to this work event coming up in a week and a half."

"Okay then. What your mom is making reference to is this work thing. That's her way of bringing us back around. She's definitely speaking about this work event. She had good multi-tasking capabilities didn't she?"

"Yes, she did."

"She's saying you do to, and that this will take you far in the situation that will be presented to you. She's saying you'll walk in someone else's shoes. My guess is Tracy that your mom is giving you a head's up that there will be an announcement of some kind at this thing. Are you up for a promotion?"

"Not that I was aware of."

"Well this is huge whatever it is. Even if what happens at the event seems insignificant at the time, whatever this is will spawn a chain of events that will lead to something big down the road, I guarantee it. At least that's what your mom is saying."

"Okay," Tracy said with a smile in her voice. She agreed to contact me in a few weeks once she had attended this work event to fill me in on the details of what took place. We hung up and I thanked her mother for visiting again and for her diligence in getting me to call Tracy so I might pass a message to her. I then went on about my business, saying to myself, "All in a day's work."

When Tracy and I traded emails a weeks later she said she did receive a small raise, which was nice! She had also given thought to what I had said about her mother showing me the riding boots, and someone putting on boots, and that her mom had told me to ask her what she was doing at 11:00AM that day. Tracy was riding her mother's horse at 11:00AM! That was the boots reference. When neither Tracy nor I understood what her mom was getting at with the boots message, her mom made reference to the time that day so Tracy would know that she saw her riding. That she was around her earlier that day, had wanted to be close to her, and so she dialed my cell phone at exactly 10:00AM my time (Central Standard Time) and 11:00AM Tracy's time (Eastern)! This scenario once again validates the power and presence of Spirit and their tremendous capability to reach out to us.

Never underestimate the strength of spirit or their ability to maneuver and manipulate things in our lives to get our attention or make things happen. I don't mean to say that they will interfere...they can't. I believe universal law in the spiritual realm dictates that they can assist us but we must experience life ourselves in order to learn life lessons we've chosen. But the strong bonds of love carry on into infinity.

The following is a reading I did with a man who came to see me at a psychic fair. What's important about this session is who comes to visit. Billy, my client, was open to anyone who might come through, but never expected to hear from his childhood friend. It was fascinating and also very touching.

"Hi Kathleen, It's very nice to meet you. My name is Billy."

"Hello Billy, I'm glad you came to see me today. Let's see who wants to connect with you today. I've got a male figure coming through...he's showing me an army sharpshooter. Does that make any sense to you? Do you know someone who is crossed that was in the Army?"

"Yes, but I'm not sure who it is yet. It could be a couple of different people."

"Well he's saying the word art now. Do you do art of some kind? Are you an artist?" Meanwhile Billy begins to shake his head indicating he isn't an artist. "Wait...he's saying that this is a name. Do you know anyone by the name, Art?"

"Oh my gosh. Yes I sure do." Billy's eyes become intent on what I'm saying. Arthur, he was a friend of mine from way back, an architect in Arizona."

"He says he's been gone for a few years now. Is that right?"

"Yes that's right."

"He's bring up the army soldier thing again Billy."

"I understand now what he means. We used to play with those small army guys when we were little. It was his set and we used to play with them often."

"Billy, Art is showing me my symbol for education. He's putting an education reference around you."

"We were in school together, in elementary school."

"Yes, but he's saying specifically teacher now. He's making a reference to one of your teachers. A female...her name starts with a P sound."

"Oh I know...he's saying B for Boosamra. One of our two teachers that year was Boosamra."

"Okay now Art is making circular motions with his hands, like drawing motions."

Billy chuckles saying, "Yes I know. We were both aspiring artists that year. We drew all the time, cartoons mostly. We would draw comic book characters."

"Now he's mentioning the name Clyde. Do you or he know a Clyde?"

"Wow, you're not going to believe this. Art used to sign his drawings with that name. He assumed the name Clyde as his pseudo. Gees."

"Art is talking now about a younger boy. Oh my....he says there was a young boy that died in the middle of town. He was riding a bike correct?"

"Yes, there was a boy who crossed at that time. A very young local boy was tragically hit and killed by a car in our small town. My, I can't believe the stuff he's bringing up!"

"He's now saying you two used to get ice cream together. He's smiling, he must have really liked ice cream" I said laughing out loud.

"Billy he is leaving now but he says thank you for making it possible for him to say hello to you."

"Thank you and him for paying me a visit. I sure am glad to hear from him. Is he alright then?"

"Yes he's fine, certainly in very good spirits."

Billy and I spoke a little while longer after our session and he reminisced about his friendship with Arthur. They met as children and remained close into adulthood. Living in separate states, Arthur had become ill and passed early in life. Billy said he would share his experience of the reading with Art's mother. I'm increasingly intrigued and amazed at the emphatic power of spirit and how they show the bonds of love keep them connected to us. Their messages, strong and intellectual are carefully chosen based on what the recipient needs to hear. Bill left me that day elated and on cloud nine.

- *The Chandelier* -

I'm often asked if spirits can see into the future. I've given you a few examples already of where I have seen they can peek and then tell when they deem it necessary for our welfare. In the case of a gal named Crystal, she had come to see me at a psychic event at one of the local hotels. Not thinking it was going to be life changing, she first sat down at my table, not really knowing anything about me or my ability. All she did know was that I was a lady on a board who was free at 1:30 for a fifteen minute reading. As Crystal sat there before me, I could feel she was ambiguous and I asked her, "Have you ever had a reading before Crystal?"

"No not a real one." By that, she meant no one had ever been accurate about her or her family who had crossed over. She was anxious to see what I had to say. Crystal considered herself an open person, and someone who believed in the process of connecting with spirit. She wanted desperately for this to be real.

"Do you have a grandmother is spirit?"

"Yes I do."

"Well your grandmother is here and she is saying hello to you. You just bought a refrigerator. She says congrats on the refrigerator." I chuckled knowing that Crystal would be shocked by that announcement.

"Yeah I did just get a new fridge two weeks ago!"

"Grandma is showing me someone else is there with her. A male figure, to your side she's saying, so that would be husband, brother, cousin…"

"My cousin is crossed over!"

"He is showing me hearts. The impression I'm getting is that it's heart related in some way. Not that this is medical, more hearts related to him. Do you understand what he's saying?"

"No honestly I don't. I'm not sure what he means."

"Crystal, your grandmother is stepping forward again and is showing me broken glass. I can hear the glass crashing and breaking. Does that mean anything to you?"

"No not really. I'm not sure what she means either."

"Well I'm not either, but I can tell you it must be important for her to bring it up. Just be careful and watch out for any broken glass crossing your path in the next few weeks okay?"

"Okay."

"You are not feeling too well are you? You have a sore throat. Your grandmother is saying you should get that looked at."

Crystal chuckles, "Gees yeah, I have a lozenge in my mouth right now!"

"Your grandmother is showing me your apartment…you do live in an apartment right?"

"Yes I do."

"It's a loft-like apartment. A loft type setting is what she's showing me."

"That's it!"

"She's showing me something loopy or looped" I said to Crystal as I made a circular and u-shaped motion in the air with my fingers to indicate to her what I was seeing.

"I'm not sure what that is, but I'll remember you said it."

"She is also giving you a 'thumbs up' regarding the man you are seeing right now. She says he's very good for you." I smiled at her grandmother's anxiousness to give Crystal approval.

"You know Crystal, you are very intuitive yourself." I can usually pick out those that will 'get it' easily and though who subconsciously fight the process. Crystal I knew would be one to pick up easily the fundamentals of the psychic senses if she pursued it. "I am going to give you a list of suggested books to read that will get you started developing your abilities." She nodded in agreement and thanked me for the list. We continued on with the reading.

"You are going to have a nontraditional Christmas this year. Have you planned anything out of the ordinary yet for the holidays?"

"Hmm…no not yet, but we'll see what happens."

"She is ready to leave now, and says she loves you very much."

"That was wonderful Kathleen, thank you so much."

With that we ended our session. Approximately two weeks later Crystal emailed me. She told me that later that day when she arrived home she recognized the message from her cousin and the hearts reference. She had found a picture of her cousin in a frame with hearts all around it. She also understood the reference her grandmother made to the looping thing in her apartment. While she was lying on her couch watching a bird out the window a few days later she noticed that her curtains make a looping shape in the way I had described. They were festoons.

Her grandmother was letting her know that she was there visiting her in her apartment. As for the nontraditional Christmas, her mother served shrimp and other fish that year, which was out of the ordinary for them. But the even bigger story was to let me know the broken glass had come to fruition that her grandmother had warned her about. Crystal and her son were walking through the hall of their apartment building and stepped through the front door. As they shut the door, both heard a tremendous sound of glass smashing on the floor. They quickly opened the door to see the damage. Broken shards of glass were spewed everywhere. In front of the entrance of her apartment door, there had been a glass light fixture. They stood there in silence. Realizing the severity of injury it could have caused either one of them had they delayed their entrance but by just a few seconds. Crystal was stunned! Her grandmother knew this was going to happen! This was the broken glass that she had warned her of. From that day Crystal said she became a true believer and would never doubt the after life and in her words "their power to help us."

I have witnessed first hand the power of spirit many times and have seen their desire to assist us in finding people and places that will make a difference in our lives. Like spiritual travel agents, they continuously monitor our voyage through life and will at times aid us in our direction. Being free will entities, it's up to us to see the often times subtle messages they send us. However, in situations where they need to make their meaning clear, they will act accordingly.

Crystal's mother came to see me several months later. Smartly she did not tell me that she was connected to Crystal prior to the reading. As far as I knew, she was just another person wanting to connect to the other side. The reading was going along very smoothly. By that I mean that the validations, names, dates and such that Crystal's mom was receiving were numerous and flowing as if I were just opening my mouth and they were speaking. Now mind you, that isn't how this usually works. Most often hearing words from spirit is like listening to talk radio on an old AM/FM Transistor low on battery power. Never the less, that day was an exception, and things like I said, were moving along nicely. I then came out with the name "Linda." No response from Crystal's mom. Then "George"...and again she had no clue who this was or what they were getting at. The reading was over shortly after that. With so many messages, she was content with the session and thanked me, then informed me of her real identity. I smiled, thanked her for being clandestine so she wouldn't impede the process, and we parted ways.

According to Crystal when I spoke to her months later, she swore she had sabotaged her mother's reading. During the reading I had told her mother of a Linda coming through. I had described this Linda to her saying she was like family to her. That this spirit was saying she was to her side (which to me means sister, friend, cousin, etc.) but that Linda was saying over and over that she was 'like family.' Linda kept asking me to say the name George as well. Come to find out, Crystal wanted confirmation that she was on the right path and pursuing the right man. Before her mom went in to have her reading that day she begged her spirit guides to please mention the name of the person whom she was thinking about in some way, and if she received this name she would know she wasn't wasting her time going after the relationship. When not one, but both of these names came out in her mom's reading, Crystal was astounded. George is the true love she hopes and believes she will one day marry. The same one her grandmother had referred to with the thumbs up. Linda was a friend of Georges' mother Ann who has crossed over! All Crystal wanted to hear was George's name. Her guides gave her that and then some! George lives in London, and Crystal came to learn about him through Ann (his mother and friend of Linda's), whom she met in a spiritual chat room. George and Linda's son were playmates as children.

Our loved ones are there, watching over us along with our guardian angels and spirit guides always. We can be certain that they care for us and that they will be dutiful in assisting us when they can. They want our journey here to be successful and just as they aided us when they were here in the physical sense, will continue their quest in the spiritual sense. The importance of this is that if we grow and learn to accept their messages and guidance, we are assured a more safe and lucrative voyage. We will spend less time fighting obstacles and more time reaping the benefits of a fruitful existence.

During a session I had with a woman named Gina, spirit showed again that for-telling the future would have an impact on the person receiving the information. The reading we had together went very well with many people coming through for Gina. However, I had mentioned that someone from the other side was insisting that there was a Margarite in her family. Gina said she didn't know for sure, but that she couldn't think of anyone at the moment. When she got home, she asked various relatives and friends, yet no one seemed to recognize a Margarite. The following weekend she attended a christening for her cousin's baby girl. While at the church she was introduced to her cousin's wife's mother. Her mouth literally fell open when they said her name, Margarite! Gina was in such astonishment that she asked her to repeat it. Once again, spirit was showing off, but also giving Gina a very influential gift of knowing how close they are to her and still connected in her daily life.

When my grandmother Claudia, my father's mother, passed away in the summer of 2002, I learned a very important lesson. Those who are skeptical here, sometimes have an awakening there on the other side. I do believe that we are supposed to forget what we 'learned' when in spirit before coming here so that our judgment isn't manipulated by preconceived notions of what we already know, but rather we take in the whole experience of these life lessons as new so we might gain facets of knowledge given specific ingredients in each lesson. My grandmother was a very spiritual woman. Claudia had many friends and her funeral became more a celebration of life, than a depressed and antiquated environment like some. I had the pleasure to muse over memories with one of her long time friends, Edith Head. I hadn't seen Edith since I was a young child. She was an actress on Broadway in her younger years and married a famous Admiral. She told me of how she loved to entertain while living in New York, and had Shirley McClain and her younger brother over many times at her soirées. She said Warren Beatty would eat almost a whole tray of croissants before she would catch him. Claudia had surrounded herself with interesting people and I must have heard a dozen times if I heard it once from folks visiting her wake, that she was the kindest and most caring person they ever met. Although you know it, those words have quite an impact on you when you hear it first hand. It was very inspiring to feel and experience the many lives my grandma had touched.

Although she was always very supportive of whatever I had done, Claudia was uncomfortable talking to me about my psychic gifts. She was glad that what I did helped others through the grieving process and that I incorporated God into my work. I had mailed a few books to her that I had hoped would spark her interest in the subject of spirit communication. My desire was that she would be able to experience what I did, and better yet, possibly even learn to receive messages from her late husband, my grandfather. When I would ask her about them on the phone, she would make excuses of being busy with other things and not having the time to 'get to them yet.' I remember my father whispering to me at his 70th birthday party as he handed the books back to me in a plastic bag, "Your grandma would prefer that you not give her any more books on this subject." At first, I was taken back. After all, she was at this party in the other room. Why didn't she just give them to me herself? After all, we were very close and always found it easy to be candid with each other. And then I stopped to consider her mortality. Her religious views went years back. She was raised to believe that you don't mess with communicating with the spirits of the dead. Once they crossed over, it was now God's job to take care of them and we were not to interfere. I decided that day to back off trying to convince my grandmother of something that she didn't care to hear about. Everyone has their own right to their belief system and it was wrong of me to try to change hers. We must all acquire our knowledge at different times, through different resources and at our own pace.

Claudia was ninety years old and in good health for someone her age. She had recently reupholstered a formal lounging chair with my mother for their living room. Something kept gnawing at me to go and visit. I live in Texas, the rest of my immediate family is in Ohio. We are a very close family and I knew my opportunities to spend time with her were dwindling with each passing year and that the inevitable would happen. She would go home soon to be with her Maker. My grandmother had just moved into my parent's house two months before, from her apartment she had had in the neighboring town. I needed to see her. My schedule was crammed and it would be very challenging to squeeze a week or so in to visit up north. The more days I procrastinated in buying airline tickets, the stronger my intuition said to buy them. I did.

In late June I went to visit and stayed with her for a week. I brought along my fifteen year old son, Chris, and two year old granddaughter, Payton. The visit was marvelous. My parent's home is so peaceful. Being surrounded by that state park creates a majestic atmosphere, and resting out on the lawn I once counted over thirty trees on their property. It's truly magical to sit in their yard on a warm summer's evening and watch as the lightening bugs create a fairy tale setting of dazzling entertainment in the twilight. One such late afternoon while my mother Mary, my grandmother, and I, sat in the back yard enjoying the breeze drinking some wine and reminiscing, I got my first sign that I was right. Payton had been playing ferociously all afternoon and had finally run out of gas, plopping down on the large covered swing my grandmother and I were sharing. She lay down resting her head in my grandmother's lap. With my mom sitting next to us in a lounge chair, my grandmother and I gently kicked our heels into the dirt in unison, rocking the swing back and forth hoping to lull Payton into a nap.

As my grandmother caressed Payton's hair, we watched as she raised her two year old hand to wave at someone seemingly off in the distance. We all immediately knew what was happening. I was the first to speak. I addressed my mom and grandmother, "Did you see that?" My mom laughed nervously, "Yeah, what was she waving at do you suppose?" My grandmother gave no response but just continued looking in the direction of where the baby waved. I then looked down at Payton and asked, "Who's out there honey? Who are you waving to?" She didn't answer and instead softly closed her eyes and drifted off to sleep. I was alarmed at what it signified and because I am not one to take things lying down, begged to ask the question again hoping to get an answer from my mom or grandma. "I wonder who she saw out there. Someone is obviously visiting us from beyond. You know how young children see things that we cannot." My mom agreed and my grandmother still had nothing to say on the subject; she was just comfortable to listen. There was nothing that even *I* could see in the yard that day. I can many times see spirit, but that day my little granddaughter was the only one (unless grandma saw them too and wasn't giving it up). My guess is, it was in preparation for what was to come just a few weeks down the road. On the last day of our trip I had been visiting my sister. When my mother and I drove back to the house around 10:00PM the front porch light was off. As we pulled onto the stone driveway we could see a silhouetted figure sitting there in the dark. "Mom, I think grandma waited up for us," I said as we got out of the car. "Your right," as she focused her eyes on the subject. "She did. I'll be darned." I had a 6:00AM flight and grandma liked to sleep in, so she had stayed up past her bedtime to say good-bye.

We walked into the house and she hugged me tight as she wished me a safe flight. I'll always remember what would be our last embrace. After a long, loving hug she gently grasped my biceps and leaning back to look deep into my eyes, she smiled and said four simple words… "I love you Kathleen." It seemed as though time had stopped. The world spinning around us, yet we didn't move a muscle. As if etched in stone, a strong memory that will stay with me forever. I smiled tenderly back at her and said, "I love you too grandma, very much." We hugged again and said good night. My second sign. She knew and I knew that would be the last time we would see each other in this lifetime. Although it was really so long and not good bye, we both sensed the finality of that encounter, yet with a deep knowing that we would reunite again.

Once home in Texas, two weeks later, I got a call from my mom telling me that my grandma was being admitted to the hospital for observation because of an obstruction in her stomach. They tried several remedies, with surgery being the last option. Other than being a little asthmatic, she was very strong. When it appeared that surgery was the only solution to deal with the obstruction, the family made plans to schedule an operation.

She was cleared for surgery. We were all nervous, given her age, but the doctors assured us that it was a fairly common procedure and that she would recover nicely and be home in no time.

The surgery took less time than originally estimated. My mom called me from recovery and had said the operation was a success. We were relieved. After being in recovery for a few hours she was transported back up to her hospital room. After that it all went downhill. Laying there one minute smiling, the next she suddenly complained of not being able to breathe. My parents were in the room, along with their friend Shirley, whom they've known for over forty years. Shirley is a retired nurse. My parents yelled for a staff nurse. When the attending nurse saw Claudia's condition, they called for a doctor stat. Ten minutes passed, no doctor. Again the nurse's station paged the doctor and again another ten minutes passed. Meanwhile my grandmother, clutching the bed sheets, had a look on her face of frustration and fear. "Why are they not coming," She asked. "Where are they, I can't breathe." My parents, now angry, started yelling at the nurses to get help in the room fast! They heard them page the doctor over and over to no avail. The pressure in her chest caused Claudia to have a stroke. We were informed later that when they inserted the main line during surgery, the surgical team punctured one of her lungs by accident. It wasn't until she was out of recovery and back in her room that her lung collapsed.

It took forty-five minutes that day for a doctor to come to the room. Not realizing the severity of the situation, he had ignored the requests for stat attention and chose to enter into a standard hernia operation with another patient instead. Those forty-five minutes made the difference between life and death for Claudia.

She had signed a DNR (a do not resuscitate order). The stroke had paralyzed her left side which removed her ability to swallow. Although able to speak in hush tones, she would now have to be put on life support to breathe properly. A DNR stops that from happening. My parents, although furious with the situation now before them, had to painfully make the arrangements for hospice care at home. A journey they knew had only one ending. Claudia remained in the hospital over the next week and they administered pain medication to her to keep her comfortable. They removed her food supply and began the process of letting her body run itself down. They would transport her via ambulance to my parent's home.

In shock at having to deal with the unexpected, my sister and two brothers and their children were thrown into a tailspin of saying last minute good-byes and assisting my parents in dealing with hospice. Shirley was a God-sent and stayed by the family's side the entire time while my grandmother deteriorated. I meanwhile, felt very helpless. I worked with people in grief every day, yet I never felt as inadequate as I did during the time my grandmother was passing. I had just been to Ohio, and wanted to fly back for the funeral. My parents had said they were unsure of how long she would live. It could be two days or two weeks. Chris was about to start school, and I had to get things in order in Texas if I was going to be gone for any great length of time. I decided to wait a week before making flight arrangements so I wouldn't have to be away from Chris. My husband and I would be going alone and Chris would start school as planned. What happened next was utterly astonishing!

A man in the desert with no food or water has approximately three days of survival. Claudia hung on without any food or water and no pain medication per her request, for nearly three weeks! Doing daily devotions and always ending in the Lord's prayer, my mother and father, along with Shirley, the hospice nurses, and my siblings would comfort her, speak with her, and even sing songs with her. Claudia would smile and you could see the profound love in her eyes as her friends came by one by one to visit and pay their last respects. She became a pillar of strength, hanging on until everyone had 'time to adjust' and 'time to say good-bye.'

You are never really ready to let a loved one go I think, no matter what the circumstances. It's our natural instinct to stay alive and keep others alive. But she gave us all a gift we will never forget. The gift of her undying love. She showed the true essence of how powerful love can really be.

The devotions were usually in the late morning. It was early and my father had gone out back to his shed to do something. My mom was making coffee in the kitchen when she saw my grandmother raise her hand in the air and wave to get her attention. They were alone in the house and she approached the hospital bed which was stationed in the living room. "What is it, mom?" my mother asked. My grandma requested they do devotions now instead of waiting for later. My mom said, "Sure," and as she turned to get my father, he walked in the house. As they each positioned themselves next to her bed, one on the right and one on the left, and started reading scripture. As they recited the Lord's prayer, her voice began to weaken, and then eventually went to a whisper. My father and mother stood there in silence as they each held one of Claudia's hands in theirs. Neither needing to speak, but watched as the volume of breathe in her chest lessened with each inhale and exhale. Claudia's chest stopped. My parents looked at each other and then back at her and my mother reached over and picked up a small mirror nearby. She gently placed the mirror under grandma's nose to check to see if she was breathing. Suddenly, my grandma took in a quick breath, almost a gasp. Then released the last bit of life force she contained in her body. It was August 3rd when she passed.

I delivered the eulogy at her funeral. As I walked to the podium in the funeral parlor with my knees shaking, my niece Courtney who was eight, jumped up from her seat in the front row and walked up next to me. She just looked up at me and smiled as if to say with her tender eyes, that everything would be all right. I smiled back at her and we wrapped our arms around one another as I proceeded to deliver what I had written on the plane in silence on my way to Ohio. There is something to be said of the wisdom of children. I normally have no problem speaking in front of groups, yet that day I was miserably nervous and outside myself, as was everyone in the immediate family. But my niece, possessing only eight years of life experience, called to action her emotions, setting aside her tears to lend her strength to me. It was just what I needed to get me through. Even the day before at the wake, my other nieces (my brother has been blessed with five girls) three under the age of seven, had shared with me while we all were gazing into the coffin that their great grandma wasn't really in that coffin. That she was in heaven and that her body lying there, was simply a shell. They were all smiling and very comforted that grandma was no longer suffering and was now in a happy place with Jesus. I know it made my grandmother proud to see her offspring so well adjusted to the dying process.

Exactly one week after arriving home in Texas, I had a psychic development class scheduled. I was anxious to jump into a routine I was familiar with and get back to some normalcy. Each member of the class is supposed to try their hand at using psychometry. We were in my office after the class and Erika, one of my students, closed her eyes as she began to sense some information coming through. She started by saying she had an older woman coming through for me and that she is 'doing this.'

Erika was motioning in the air and taking her index finger and scraping at the cuticle of her thumb as if picking at it. Then she said just that.

"Kathleen she is doing this for me, like she's picking at her thumb."

I about fell off my chair. There was only one person I knew who that belonged to. The characteristic was so precise that I knew immediately who it was that was coming through. It was the one red flag that would be a sure fire sign. My grandmother had a nervous condition or a *tick* as some people refer to it. She would pick at her thumb with her index finger constantly. I couldn't believe that Claudia of all people was coming through!

"Now she's showing me paralysis. She's also showing me a very large picture window. It's very bright."

"I know who it is Erika and I understand what it is that she's showing you. Go on, please."

Erika now had her eyes open and seemed comfortable with the process and what was happening. She kept moving forward. "Now she is saying her left arm is swollen. That she is experiencing pain in her left arm. She had a heart attack or stroke didn't she? She's making my chest all warm."

"Yes, she sure did. What else is she saying?"

"Under her eyes it's very puffy. She had pretty eyes, but they are puffy underneath."

"Right, exactly, she had quite large bags under her eyes."

"She is showing me an ambulance."

"Yes I understand that. It has to do with them moving her after her paralysis."

"She's showing me a big man with a round puffy face."

"Yes, that's her husband."

"She now has crocheted things around her. Did she crochet?"

"Oh yes, she did all types of needle work. She loved to crochet."

"But she is being specific about what she is showing me. This is a special blanket. It has variegated colors of brown, yellow and orange. She has it over her knees."

With that, I broke down and started to cry. As much as I tried to compose myself I just couldn't believe that my grandma was being so clear and loud and definitive in her messages to me. She was afraid of this 'psychic stuff' when she was here. She never embraced it like I would have liked. It was difficult for her to justify changing her belief system after so many years. What it boiled down to is she wasn't taking any chances in making God angry with her. She knew she'd be 'going home' soon and wanted to make sure heaven's door was open for her. I had sent her books and videos on the subjects of the afterlife and speaking to the other side, but she returned them to me saying she was supportive of what I did if it was helping others, but that she had no interest! I decided that I shouldn't and wouldn't push my beliefs on her. We just agreed to disagree and left it at that. In my experience as a medium I have seen it common that those who are skeptical here on the earthly plane are many times the first to come through in a reading from the other side. To have this happen to me though, and it be so personal was overwhelming.

My grandmother had kept the blanket Erika was describing over her couch for many years. She had crocheted it herself when my grandfather was still alive. Before I left Ohio, my mother had given me that blanket, along with a green cape to have in memory of her. Erika continued.

"She' showing me the stitch, it's a shell like design."

"Erika...she is describing it to a tee. I'll show it to you after we finish. It's downstairs in my living room."

"Holy cow, you're kidding."

"No I'm not kidding." I said smiling. "What else does she have to say?"

"Well, now she is saying that she is sitting in the dark. I don't know what that means, but just that she is sitting in this place in the dark all by herself."

"I know what she is talking about. She's referring to the last night I saw her alive. She waited for me in the dark on my mom's porch."

"She has a lot of white hair! It's very soft looking and fluffy. She had thick hair didn't she?"

"Yes she did."

"Hmmm...she is saying that she is living somewhere but that it is not her house, yet she has her own furniture in this house. Does that make sense?"

"Perfect sense," I said smiling.

"She shows me that she is sitting up in a chair yet she is paralyzed on her left side. She says there is an old fashioned looking lamp and table covered with a pink cloth from her house next to the chair where she is sitting."

I put my hands over my mouth! My mom had told me of how they propped grandma up in the chair at her request so when her friends came to see her she wouldn't look so pathetic. They used a pillow to keep her sitting upright. The lamp and table, including the pink cover, was indeed brought from her home and placed in my parent's living room when she had moved in. They wanted her to feel as comfortable as possible and had gotten rid of some of their own living room furniture to make room for hers. I couldn't speak. I just nodded my head as Erika went on.

"She says there is a tingling in her left side. Not pain, just a slight tingly feeling. She can't feel much. She's showing me her face is lucid."

"I understand. She's saying that even though she was paralyzed, she was aware of what was happening."

"She's doing this," Erika does arm movements as if hugging herself. "She is like…wrapping something around you. Did she wrap you in a blanket?"

I knowingly smiled and said, "No, she is talking about her cape my mom gave me. I wore her cape home on the plane. It felt so good to curl up in it on the ride home. It felt like a blanket. She's just letting me know she saw I have it. That's nice."

"She is leaving but she wants me to say one more thing."

"What is it Erika?"

"Well, I don't want to be wrong. This is so sensitive. But she is really making it strong so I feel I have to say it."

Perplexed I urged her to go on.

"This is your grandmother isn't it? She wants me to say that she is your grandmother."

I sat there dumbfounded. I knew who we were speaking with. But for her to make Erika 'say it' was the biggest validation I received! I felt it was her way of saying to me, "I know you know, but I will show you that I now understand what it is that you do and how you do it. I want to acknowledge for you the bonds of love you provide to others every day in your work. Thank you for doing this. This is my way of rewarding you." She knew I'd be skeptic, even though I believed in the process, I wanted and needed that last validation from her. I think she knew even more than I knew myself! With that, Erika finished the reading and I left the class that night both exhausted and elated! My life forever changed by the love of my grandmother!

~ *What You Perceive You Can Achieve.*
Discovering a Unique Ability ~

The practice of communicating with spirit allows me to learn a great deal about how the other side works. I don't preach to know all the answers, but we mediums do come to understand after repeated nuances, certain things in the afterlife that are steady and unwavering. When a person comes to me for a reading, they generally are interested in making a connection with specific individuals in spirit. Although I can't guarantee who will visit them during the session, in my quest to fulfill their need to make that connection with their special loved one, I try my absolute best to bring through from the other side, those they wish to hear from. I seem to have an extremely high success rate at this, roughly ninety percent of time I can make it happen.

During readings I can usually tell if I have not connected with the person on the other side my client was hoping to hear from. I had counseled them before the reading to please remain open to who ever might come through and to respect the extraordinary amount of energy it takes for spirits to reach us from the other side. Having experienced great loss myself, I understood the frustration and anguish they experience when not making that connection in a reading. I informed them that towards the end of the session, if we hadn't connected with who they desired to hear from, then I would at that point ask my client the nature of their relationship to the deceased (brother, sister, lover, etc.) but not their name and I would attempt to bring them through. I am astonished at how frequently this seems to work. By the mere fact of asking my guides for help and knowing the relationship to my client, their specific spirits come through. And these are not minor validations we receive, but rather what ensues is a substantial amount of information (including names, dates, etc,) and a reading that turns from 'okay' to 'outstanding'!

One of the first readings I experienced like this was conducted for a man named Andre. He was very familiar with metaphysical studies and was already educated on how the process works of speaking to spirit. We met through a mutual acquaintance. When he arrived for his appointment, he was very relaxed and anxious to get started. He had told me up front that there was one specific individual he was hoping to hear from but that he would be appreciative of anyone who came through to visit him. I didn't realize it at the time, but he had even brought a picture of this person and had it lying on the floor next to his chair on the other side of the desk across from me. When we began our session, several people came through for him. One significant person was an old Army buddy he had served with in the Gulf War. He was happy yet somewhat surprised that this man would show up in his reading. His friend had thanked him for the camaraderie and support Andre had bestowed on him when he was alive and gave Andre several validations to let him know that he was around and aware of what was taking place in Andre's life. After about forty minutes into the reading, I asked Andre if there was someone he would like to connect with that hadn't happened yet. He replied there was and said that his grandfather was someone who he had really hoped to hear from.

Almost immediately his grandfather Nigel identified himself and said that he was responsible for raising Andre. Andre was elated and excited to see what else his grandfather would have to say and asked me to proceed. Nigel went on to say that he knew Andre had had one son, that he was six years old, and that he had won several awards from participating in Karate events. He told Andre that he knew of his divorce and then comforted him by recognizing also that Andre had custody of his son and said he was doing a fantastic job of raising him alone with high morals and values. Nigel even described what he was wearing in a picture that Andre had brought to the session. There were many insights Nigel gave Andre that day, too many to mention, but the point is that when we asked to reach Nigel, he did in fact oblige and come through. Needless to say, I was very thankful and happy that Andre got to experience again the seemingly strong relationship between him and his grandfather by making that connection.

A short time later I did a reading for a woman named Patricia. She had recently lost her husband and had called me, desperate, seeking closure concerning how he died. The coroner had ruled his death accidental, but she was convinced that events leading up to his passing were clandestine and that the authorities had missed something during their investigation. She sounded very urgent and it so happened that I had just received a cancellation for an appointment two days later. She took it. When she arrived at my office the day of her reading she was visibly nervous and I suggested we do some breathing exercises prior to the session to calm her. I tried to reassure her that regardless of how he passed he was in a safe place now and was content and happy. Those words seemed to provide a small amount of peace and we proceeded with the reading. At first her father-in-law came though. He spoke of disappointment in missing so much of his life experience here on earth having died at an early age. He noted that she was about to go back to school to take a pottery class, one of her many hobbies. He announced that he had someone 'under' him there with him on the other side and that he was assisting this person through. Patricia began to shift in her seat and became acutely attentive to my next words. I told her it was a male with her father-in-law and that I was hearing the name Jeff. "That's him!" She yelled.

Jeff said that he had been trying very hard to let her know of his presence around her, and had tried to give her several signs that he was near. He told her of how he touched her shoulder as she picked from his closet the clothes she would put on him at his funeral. Patricia began to sob and agreed that she had felt a gentle squeeze on her right shoulder that day. She felt it was Jeff making contact with her, but then assumed she was just feeling this because of her strong sense of wanting it to happen so badly. She thanked him during the reading for acknowledging this. He also said he had appeared in the cemetery. When I asked him in what way, he answered that he had manifested as ecto (the white or sometimes grey, smoky substance appearing like fog) at the burial service. Patricia gasped. She explained that one of her dear friends had mentioned after the service, seeing something that appeared to be a misty like substance hovering over the gravesite.

Patricia left my office that day uplifted and with a renewed sense of closeness to her deceased husband. She shared with me just as she was about to walk out the door, "I'm so thankful that Jeff came through for me today. I was so worried not enough time had passed since he's been gone and that he wouldn't have the strength to come through. The funeral was only last week!" I looked at her dumbfounded. Trying to hide my shock I responded with, "Well it just goes to show you how the bonds of love make anything possible. He must have loved you tremendously to work that hard to not only give you signs, but to then elicit the help of his father in assisting him with the ability to come through. I do believe, Patricia, you can feel certain that his father was there to greet him when Jeff crossed over." What a great day that was for both of us.

I believe that 'what you perceive, you can achieve.' I have consistently found after many readings that we can call upon specific souls and make that connection. The caveat of whether they respond still seems to be that if the recipient (the person I'm reading for) is supposed to get a message from that specific soul, that spirit will come through. If they are not supposed to get a message from that specific soul, for reasons known only in the spirit world, we will not be able to make that connection with that particular soul. I still believe we only get the messages we are supposed to have. There is a much higher power in control. Spirits can see into the future and know much better than we that life is exponential and that based on what happens today, will dictate what takes place tomorrow. Spirits, I'm sure, use this reasoning when deciding who receives which messages from whom. But it's comforting to me to recognize and comprehend that I can take mediumship to the next level and more often than not, make a connection happen between a loved one who's crossed and their counterpart still here on the earthly plane.

When discussing mediumship and everything that is the spirit realm, I can understand why skeptics might choose to believe that it's a person's desire that convinces them they are communicating with the other side. Yet, I have seen time and again where there is absolutely no room left for doubt in the specific and irrefutable information that comes from a source that we as humans cannot see, touch, or feel in a physical and tangible sense but rather a source that is spiritual and from a realm other than our own. The undeniable truth is that I am certain of two things in my work as a medium. One, that I am working with God and in Godly light in all that I do, and two, that I truly am in touch with those loving souls in the afterlife who make contact with us for the sole purpose of telling us that they still exist. Life is eternal and they will prove it to us when we allow ourselves to be open to hearing from them. We each must make our own decisions regarding our belief system and cultivate our own personal relationship with our Maker. When we ourselves cross over into the spiritual heavens we will be asked to examine our life spent here on earth. It's then that we will assess our goals and achievements as souls. We will be assigned the task of evaluating ourselves. Our Maker will not judge us, but instead He will have us judge ourselves. I believe it's up to us to make the most out of each lifetime and to utilize all that God gave us to work with while here.

If we choose to live happier, fulfilled and productive lives by facing and moving past our illusions, fears, doubts and blockages of love, we will make great strides in accomplishing our goals on a soul's level. As you open yourself up spiritually, life's path will gradually get easier and less convoluted with emotional baggage from the past (including past lives) and become more clear, concise, and comprehensible with what God's plan is for you. How do you do this? You build a strong relationship with your Maker and your higher consciousness. Through daily meditation, prayer and visualization you increase your vibrations to meet a spiritual plane that you will know exists and is as much a part of you as the earthly plane. Esoterically they call it 'becoming one with the universe.' My hope is that you will find as I did, that we are all part of the same body, all a part of God, and so, we share many more similarities as people than we do differences.

We are all pieces of energy. Everything we do, think, say, and feel becomes impressed on our aura and on the wall of the universe as well. A good example of this is an incident that took place in my kitchen a while back. My friend Marco and I were channeling for each other. I had brought through an uncle for him who had died a torturous death. Out of respect for Marco I won't go into detail. The point is that his uncle had come through with specific validations surrounding his death experience which in turn answered questions for Marco. Although it was sad circumstances, the reading itself went well. Sitting at the end of my kitchen table, Marco's chair was positioned next to the windows. When it was Marco's turn to read for me, he immediately pointed to the window on his left and said, "What is this...this right here? A young boy died there?" Naturally he was puzzled, but not doubting the information he was receiving, he continued. "I'm feeling that a young boy died there, right outside this window!" I knew right away what he was referring to. I wanted all of the information to come from the person in spirit who was talking to Marco, therefore I refrained from pontificating and just told Marco that he was right in what he was asking me, but to please give me more. What else was the young boy saying to him?

Marco continued by lifting his right arm, bent at the elbow, and starting swinging it letting his hand fall back and forth, left to right as in a dangling motion. "He is showing me swinging...something is swinging like this." Again, making the movement with his arm. "Kat, he's saying that's how he died!" "That's right," I said. "Go on. What else is he saying?" Marco then put his hands around his throat and said, "Oh my, he was strangled? He says that's what caused his passing. He's making me feel tightness around my throat." I nodded in agreement.

I explained to Marco that it was Baron, a friend of my son Chris, who was giving him the messages. I told him how Chris had attended a birthday party and as the kids arrived, they were told that their friend Baron had hung himself accidentally with his Karate belt. He had been playing around in his room and one end of the belt became wrapped around the ceiling fan, the other around his neck. He became unconscious and although the family heard the commotion, found him almost immediately after it happened and got medical attention, Baron went into a coma and never recovered. He died in the hospital several days later. The kids were sent home from the birthday party and when Chris walked through the back gate of our yard you only had to look at his face to know something was very wrong. I happened to be outside in the yard when he came home. I approached him concerned and asked what was wrong. Chris started to cry and said, "Come with me." I followed him across our pond and onto the side of the house to a private patio. He sat on a window ledge (which is only a foot off the ground) and told me what had happened to Baron.

When Marco first began the reading he had picked up on the energy impressed on that window ledge. Even though more than two years had passed since that fateful day when Chris relayed the horrible news of Baron's passing, the intense energy of that pain was still present in that area.

Be cautious and responsible with what you think, say and do, because you too leave an impression of energy on the universe. When I first learned of energy impressions I became a better driver. I have always said I must have been in the short line when they handed out patience because I possess very little. I am born in a generation of instant gratification and I, like most people, am moving at warp speed most of the time. A road rage devotee I'm not, but I used to have a short fuse when driving in traffic and spoke frequently under my breath at the person in front of me to 'get a move on!' I probably caused a lot of headaches. I now try to drive in a much calmer state and am careful not to think or speak, even to myself, negative thoughts regarding others.

One of my goals in writing this book is to get you to consider new ways of thinking. By sharing with you stories of my experiences communicating with the other side and experiencing spirit at work, I hope through those personal interpretations you'll find enlightenment. My observation of energy as a whole is that we influence the universe and the universe influences us! The laws of physics apply here. For every action there must be an equal and opposite reaction. Although what I do for a living may be considered entertainment by some, there is actual science involved, in and throughout the combination of the earthly and spiritual planes. Take sensing ability in animals for instance. It's a clear sunny day and horses in a pasture begin to become restless. They start running in various directions, then stopping short as if waiting for something, and then start to run again. The rancher, who owns the horses, sees they are anxious and begins to gather the horses and secure them in the stable. Suddenly out of nowhere, the sky becomes a dark grey and within minutes a tornado is blowing by overhead. Although the rancher had no warning, and never sensed a change in the weather coming, the horses instinctively knew imminent danger was approaching. Why are animals able to see and sense things that we cannot? Because they are attuned to their senses and use all of what God gave them at all times. We should learn a lesson here. We are no different, and should and can tap into all the gifts He gave us for living on this linear plane.

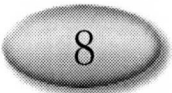

~ How Spirit Teaches Us ~

In the many sessions I've had and the clients I've encountered, each of them has offered answers to the dynamics by which spirit works and the limitless capabilities we possess once on the other side. Do we exist on a specific plane for a certain period of time after we cross? Can a spirit be in two places at the same time? Do we hold on to our personalities that were part our physical existence? How do we know when our loved ones who have passed are around us? There are a plethora of questions beckoned to be answered. My official response when asked many of these questions is this… 'The earthly plane is school.' We are in training here and it is our destiny to learn and fulfill the life lessons chosen by us before possessing a physical existence. Although I believe that those close to us who are now in spirit form have the ability to see into the future, it is important for them to not give us all the answers. To certainly not make things easy for us, for then we would not learn but rather become lazy souls, repeating the same mistakes and expecting different outcomes. Through my experiences working with spirit I will attempt to answer some of the mysteries surrounding the differences between the physical and spiritual realms and you draw your own conclusions based on the evidential readings I am about to share with you. I have shortened many of these sessions to exclude the superfluous parts, but include the validations that tell the story of these differences.

- Spirit can be in two places at the same time -

During a phone reading I did with a woman by the name of Tracy, two interesting things took place which authenticated for me, something I learned about the powers of those in the beyond. The following is an excerpt from that session.

"Good evening Tracy"

"Hello Kathleen...listen, we may have a slight problem with this reading tonight."

"Why is that?"

"Well, my stepfather just emailed me and informed me that he too has hired a medium for this evening to try to connect with my mother. That is who I was hoping to connect with as well. Is this going to be a problem? How can my mother be in two places at the same time?"

"Tracy, I don't think this will be a problem. First of all, I've seen spirits have tremendous power. Their delineation of space and time is something we cannot quite comprehend. Those in spirit are not governed by the same boundaries we experience here. Although I can't promise who will come through tonight, if your mom wants to get a message to you, she will, trust me. I also believe we get the messages we are supposed to have when we are supposed to have them. Most spirits are meticulous when choosing the way they deliver their messages."

We both laughed at the precariousness of the situation and agreed that we would forge ahead and see what would take place. What proceeded was not only her mom being in two places at the same time, but also letting Tracy know personally that she was aware of her concerns.

"Okay then Tracy, let's get started. I have a male figure coming through. He says that he is to your side, so that to me would be brother figure, friend, and husband, someone in that category. Do you have a male friend who has crossed over?"

"Yes I do."

"Okay, he is saying now that this was an intimate relationship but not romantically involved. Does that make sense for you?"

"Yes it does, go on."

"He is saying that someone else died near the time of his death also. Is that true?"

"Yes, yes that's right."

"Tracy he says he has the person that passed around the time of his death with him. That they are together there. He did not know this person when here in the physical world though correct? That is what he is saying."

"Yes, that's correct. They didn't know each other. I can't believe that they are together up there!"

"Well he is saying that he wants full credit for bringing this female in to speak with you. I am getting that this is your mom, but she will give us details to validate that it is her."

"Wow, I can't believe this."

"Mom says that she died of an illness is that right?"

"Yes, that's right."

"And this illness was a very lengthy process. She says it dragged out for some time."

"Yes it did."

"Tracy, she is mentioning the name Sandy. Does that mean anything to you?"

"No, not that I can think of."

"Hmm…well she is making it bigger for me, so she knows what she wants to say. Think for a moment, this could be a friend as well as a relative, and it could be for her or for you."

Tracy thought for a moment, but failed to recollect anyone with that name who she could associate with. As Tracy was pondering the name, her eyes fell on the monitor of the computer sitting in front of her. The email her stepfather sent her announcing he also was seeing a medium that night was still on her screen.

"Whoa...wait a minute Kathleen. I think I know what she is referring to now. Gees, okay, yeah I know a Sandy. That is the name of the medium my dad is meeting with right now."

"Is that right!? Well, guess mom has a sense a humor, eh?" We both laughed.

Tracy's mom took the opportunity to let her know that she knew of her stepfather's meeting with the other medium and that her name was Sandy. When Tracy spoke with her stepfather later, he told her that her mother had given him many validations also and that his late wife had come through for him too.

We associate space and time in a dimension that is limited to our knowledge of what we can see and touch. The spiritual realm operates from a perspective of what is unseen and unheard. If a blind person is asked to picture a door in his mind, does he not see it? Even if blind since birth, he will create some type of manifestation in his mind as to what a door means to him based on what he has developed using his other senses. Where is the beginning and end of a circle once the two ends meet? Is the beginning not now the end and end not now the beginning? In the universe, just as in the laws of physics, all is measurable but at the same time eternal. Everything in the universe is about balance. So is communication with the other side. The point here is that spirits can be in multiple places simultaneously. You have to open your mind to the possibilities of what it is that they actually are capable of. Remember, you too will some day have those capabilities again. Here is more from that same reading where Tracy's mom let's her know that she is around her and still sees what is going on in her family's life.

"Your mom is showing me a blanket used to cover her. She's saying that there is something special about it."

"Yes, it's true. There is something significant about the blanket."

"She is also saying that there is something significant about the date on which she died. It's also someone's birthday or anniversary?"

"Yes, that's right."

"Your mom is playing the song 'Suzy Q' for me. That must mean something to you? Or is there a Suzie she's trying to make reference to?"

"No there is no Suzy that I know of. And the song doesn't hold any special meaning for me."

"Well just remember she is making reference to that song and write it down in your notes. I'm sure she is saying it for a reason. She's making it louder so that's her way of letting me know she knows what she wants to say, we're just not able to validate it at the moment."

"Okay, I'll write it down."

In this reading Tracy's mom went on to give her many details of birthdays, anniversaries, and other information that validated for Tracy she was indeed communicating with her mom. The next day when telling her oldest daughter of what took place in the session, she described how her mom was playing the song 'Suzy Q' for her. Her daughter's eyes opened wide as she yelled out that just the day before, she and her sister were in the kitchen when that song came on the radio. They had belted it out, singing along with the song 'Suzy Q.'

- Spirit can look into the future giving us messages at the proper time that we should have them. -

Because spirits who have crossed over possess the ability to see into the future, I've said they show they are very selective in when and why they give specific messages. I've seen many times where spirits will give information to their loved ones here that at the time of the session seems insignificant or something they cannot validate or understand. Yet, at a later date it will not only make sense, but will also be a confirmation that they are around us, and are still enjoying a spiritual relationship with us. The impact of these messages hold many reasons as to why they come to pass at later dates; sometimes because the messages are to be shared with others, sometimes because it will be at a time when the person who received the message is in a better frame of mind to accept whatever messages are being delivered. The fact remains, that spirits know when and why. They possess the wisdom to bring about the cause and effect of their messages. Some examples of this are from a second session I had with Tracy months later and also in a session I had with a woman named Marilyn. In Tracy's case, she had asked in her first reading if during our session she could make a request to the male figure we were connecting with. She wanted her best friend to make reference to the nick name he used to call her. At the time he would only say *wild thing*. Tracy said that was 'close' but would like his response to be a little more specific. If he would only say the actual name, she suggested, she could then believe it was truly him. But the male figure would only repeat the words *wild thing* in the form of the song with the same name. A few months later in our second reading together, Tracy explained the following scenario to me.

"My stepfather Bill with whom I am very close, came to visit me over the Christmas holiday. I was showing him around the house and taking him throughout the rooms. When we stepped into one of my daughter's bedrooms there is an area with many stuffed animals. We picked up one of the animals and were looking at it. While midstream in conversation, I squeezed the animal to show my stepfather it plays a song. As the music began, I immediately thought back to the reference made by my male friend in our first reading when I asked him to tell me my nickname. The song exuding from the plush toy was 'Wild Thing!'"

"Wow, isn't that something!" Elated that she was able to make a connection with the information her friend had said.

"The real 'kicker' Kathleen is that the animal is a stuffed monkey. The nickname he used to call me is MONKEY!"

It wasn't until months later that Tracy was given that validation of the nickname, a time when Bill would enjoy the validation as well. Based on what was happening in Bill's life at that time, this large act of spirit, may have been what was needed to encourage him in continuing his pursuit into understanding what lies beyond. Loved ones in spirit have precise reasons for dishing out the information they do. Know that what they do is not random, but an intricate weave of testimony and scholarship in assisting us with growth here in the physical realm.

Marilyn's story is interesting from another perspective. Marilyn was what we call a skeptic. A strong Christian, she was very unsure of what purpose it would serve to visit me. At her daughter's urging, she finally mustered up the courage to call my office and arrange an appointment to meet with me. She had told me over the phone her feelings about seeing a medium, and that she was coming reluctant and not knowing what to expect. I explained to her that I felt it was healthy that she be skeptical and promised that she wouldn't be disappointed if she would only come with an open mind. When Marilyn arrived at my office she was visibly uncomfortable and nervous. Trying to make her feel more secure I gently invited her in and we then spoke for some time about how the process of connecting with someone in spirit works. When I felt she was ready, we began the session. Here is a portion of what took place.

"Marilyn I have a male coming through who says he's to your side, so to me that means, husband, brother, cousin, friend...he says he's your husband. Is your husband deceased?"

"Yes he is."

"He is showing me discomfort in his chest area. He passed from a heart attack or stroke correct?"

"Yes, yes he did."

"This was a sudden passing he's saying, it was unpredicted."

"Yes that's right."

Marilyn got emotional at this point and I could feel her tensing up. I continued.

"He says that it was his time to go. He would've liked to have stayed longer but knew it was time for him to leave. He was an outdoors type wasn't he?"

"Yes he was. He loved the outdoors."

"He's showing me Branson, Missouri. Did you two go there to watch the shows?"

"Yes, yes we did. We had such a good time there."

"He is showing me 'Austin Powers'...the movie...does that mean anything to you?"

"No, can't say that it does. We never went to see any of the 'Austin Powers' movies."

"Hmmm, well he's repeating it again, but not attaching any other emotion with it, so other than the exact meaning, I don't think he means someone else named Austin or something along those lines. Well just remember I said that. He's being specific about 'Austin Powers' and is showing it to me again. Maybe it will come to you later. Who is Rusty or sounds like Russ?"

"That's my husband's name, Russ."

"He is also showing me a 'D' name. He's trying to make reference to the male 'D' name in the family."

"I understand. There are two 'D' names, both his grandchildren."

"He's showing me a cross he wants me to mention. He says you have a cross in your house?"

"No...not that I can think of. There are no crosses in my home."

"Are you sure...think about it. He's says yes, that there is a cross attached to your home somewhere. This is very important he's saying."

"Honestly Kathleen, I cannot think of any cross in my house right now."

"That's okay. Just remember he's mentioning it. Maybe it will come to you later. Do you know why he would be showing me the Rivera Hotel?"

"Yes.....we went to Las Vegas five or six years ago and stayed at the Rivera Hotel. The room was wonderful and we had such a good time there!"

"Well, he's bringing that up and reminding you of this great memory. Now he's showing me a vase with small glass marbles or pieces of glass in the bottom...you know to hold the flower stems in place?"

"Yes, I know what you mean. I have a vase like that in my dining room."

"Marilyn, do you work with animals? Like in a clinical setting, a vet clinic, or are you a volunteer for the humane society? Russ is making me feel that there is an animal/clinical reference connected to you in some way."

"Not me. I don't do that type of work for a living. I take care of my daughter's dog. Is that what he's saying?"

"No, that's not it. He's correcting me saying that it is more clinical. It's something else. I'm going to just leave that with you because that's all I'm getting with that. He says it's connected to you and it's someone who works with animals in a clinical setting, okay?"

"Okay."

Shortly after that exchange, our session ended. Marilyn was both amazed and comforted by what had taken place. She thanked me sincerely and then left for home. A few days later I received this email from her, excitedly sharing with me the events that had followed our meeting.

"Hi Kathleen:

I am emailing you to tell you what has taken place since I met with you last week. Here goes....You asked me if I liked 'Austin Powers' because Russ was showing you the name of 'Austin Powers.' I told you neither I nor my husband liked 'Austin Powers' and you said the spirit was showing that name and I should write it down. So I did. I have never watched a movie with him in it. Now Chris and Susan (my daughter and her boyfriend) had walked to Blockbuster Video while I was at church so that Dustin (Russ' grandson) could pick out a movie. Chris said as soon as he walked through the door he asked for a certain movie. When I saw the video sitting on the coffee table I picked it up and looked at the title. It was 'Austin Powers' in *"The International Man of Mystery."* Of course I watched the movie but was up and down missing some of it. When I finally sat down to watch the movie it looked like at times it was being filmed in Las Vegas. To top it off, after about fifteen to twenty minutes, it showed the Rivera Hotel where Russ and I stayed when we were there! In detail it showed the big red lights identifying the hotel 'RIVERIA.' I could not believe what I was seeing. Susan and Chris did not know anything about you mentioning 'Austin Powers' until I picked up the movie and read the title. You had also asked me if there was a cross in our house or if I knew of one. At the time I told you I did not remember a cross in my home. Well guess what? Chris and Dustin were out in front of our house Sunday and Chris found a cross out in the front yard! On the front of the cross there is an inscription of "God loves you." On the back, it has John 3.16. It was not attached to a chain because it didn't have a loop on it. All it was is a little inexpensive cross. But it meant so much to me when I saw it. I know that was Russ' way of saying God loves me and he does too! Chris placed the cross next to the vase where I have the little glass cuttings to hold the flowers that you had mentioned in the reading also. This morning while I was in my bath room, I picked up a church bulletin which I get each week from my son's church. It was folded in half and all that showed was "*Work With Animals.*" When I opened it up the complete title was "*Senior Wants To Work With Animals.*" This article was about a high school senior, Brandy, who attends my son's church in Sherman. She thinks she might like to be a zookeeper when she grows up. That is if she decides not to become a marine biologist. You were shown that someone loved animals. And that they were connected in some way to our family. I told Russ today, after I found the bulletin, that he was driving me crazy and I know he is having fun doing it. Plus I told him he is laughing at me every time something comes up that you had mentioned. You know he was a practical joker and he used to have so much fun with me doing crazy things. If his spirit is playing with me I love it. It makes me realize he has not left me at all. Thank you so much for everything you have given me because it has helped me in so many ways.

Marilyn"

    To reiterate, what this shows us is that people in spirit have the ability to give us what we need to make us understand that they are truly still connected to us. Based on our needs and how we process information, each spirit will deliver to us the messages necessary to convey the meanings they wish to get across. Here are answers to other common questions about the experience of souls after they cross over.

- How do souls that were in conflict while on earth such as suicide, act out their existence once they cross over? -

This is actually a general question but has many answers. People who take their own life do not elevate quickly like others. They must sometimes re-live their experience of death until they understand it, or are sometimes given opportunities to "make up for their mistake" by doing deeds for others who are still here on earth. For instance, I had a client come to me hoping to hear from a grandparent who had crossed. Instead, when she first sat in my office, the individual who came through was a friend of her sister's who had committed suicide. He had been a famous DJ in Connecticut. He described to her through me, how he died. I immediately felt a wave of deep depression come over me. He told in detail what his funeral was like, and how there had been a very long procession of cars, and the many people who had visited his wake. He requested that she take back with her, an apology to his wife, his children and his family for leaving them the way he did. He stated that he knew now that suicide wasn't the answer and that because he was able to pass on these messages, learn from his death experience, and help others on the other side, he was very happy now. Once he said those things he allowed her grandparent to come through. This woman was shocked. This DJ was the last person she would have expected to hear from. But she was glad that she had been given the opportunity to pass on such an important message to her sister's friend.

I possess clairsentience, which means I have the ability to experience physically and emotionally what the spirits are feeling. I can tell you...I felt the depression early on in the ding which made me realize it was a suicide which then made possible the ability to describe in detail to this woman how he died. But more importantly, towards the latter part of the reading, I could feel that he was so happy and content and would work diligently to try to keep others from making the same mistake. Just as in physical life, people and spirits are free will entities. Some people learn quickly, some don't. It takes some souls longer to adjust after crossing over, others not so long.

- What about a soul that was ill on earth? -

Souls that were ailing, whether physical or mental, from multiple sclerosis to alzheimer's disease, pretty much seem to be back in optimum form once they cross to the other side. Again keep in mind, their willingness to be accepting of information, growth, and desire to achieve and excel will dictate their level of graduation to other dimensions. Personalities tend to stay in tact even after physical death. A woman by the name of Dana visited me with the desire of connecting with her mother. As Dana took a seat in front of me I could see she felt uneasy and tenuous. I had noticed her hand was cold when I shook it and it was seventy-five degrees outside. I asked her if she had ever visited a medium before and she said yes, but that she hadn't been successful yet in connecting with the person she was hoping to. I informed her that her relaxing would help the process and to try to be open to whomever paid us a visit. I explained to her that sometimes those we least expect show up, yet lead in those we desire to hear from. At that prospect, Dana seemed to settle in more and was eager now to get on with the session. Here is what transpired that spring day in my office.

"Dana, I have a male figure that is above you coming through and he says he's your grandfather. Do you have a grandfather in spirit?"

"Yes, yes I do."

"He's saying he crossed a long time ago is that right?"

"Yes...I didn't know him too well."

"He's claiming that he has the same first name as someone else in the family."

"Yes he does." Dana smiled then shifted in her chair to be more comfortable.

"He says that he lived nearby then had to move quite a distance from you."

"Yes that's true."

"He is saying that August is an important birthday to you, is that right?"

Dana gasped and threw her right arm across her chest. "Yes!"

"He is your mom's father isn't he? He is claiming to have his daughter there with him."

"Yes, August is my mother's birthday month."

Dana starts clapping with joy. I am overwhelmed by her mother's love coming through and begin to describe as best I can, the feelings her mother is giving me.

"Dana...your mother loves you so very much. She said it was important for her to not come through to you until now. She said she feels you are more adjusted now and have become more at ease with the fact that she is in spirit. She says that had she come to you earlier, you might not have accepted the information she would give you. That you would have only accepted the words you wanted to hear, instead of what she wanted to say. Does that make sense to you?"

"Yes totally. I understand what she is saying. She knows I am more open now because I have dealt with the grief. I have resolved myself to the truth about a lot of things. I've come to some clear answers about my own mortality."

"She's telling me Rose. Do you know a Rose? Oh wait, she is shaking her head 'no' for me. She's correcting me and saying that it's her name. Her name was Rose wasn't it?"

Dana starts to cry but is smiling with happiness. I reach across my desk and hand her a tissue.

"Rose, yes that is her name, thank you. You don't know how important that was for me to hear you say her name."

"Rose is saying that she suffered a great deal while she was here. She was bed ridden for some time is that right?"

"Yes she was."

"She had difficulty walking she says."

"Yes, she couldn't walk anymore towards the end of her illness."

"But she says she loved to dance while here. Just so you know she is showing me that she is dancing. She's twirling around with her arms outstretched. She says she can dance again and it makes her so happy."

"You're kidding!" Dana creases her brow in surprise. I start to chuckle because her mom is becoming so animated.

"I'm serious! She was a very funny lady too she says, quite the practical joker."

Dana begins laughing. "That's so true, she was always so jovial."

"Dana she says you are worried about her condition, whether or not she is okay."

"Yes, of course, does she seem alright?!"

"Dana, she's more than alright. She wants you to know that she has none of the limitations she had while here. She says that she chose those lessons herself, and that she learned a lot from her experiences. She had cancer correct? She says she went through chemotherapy and had lost her hair."

"Yes!"

"She cared about the way she looked too. She was what most people would consider vain. Always dressed impeccable she says, everything matching, shoes, purse, etc."

"Yes, yes that was her. Always dressed to the nines! It was so hard for us to see her in that condition."

"She's thanking you for the hat. She says the beautiful hat you placed on her head gave her back her dignity. It meant a lot to her that you did that."

"Oh my gosh." Dana said as she covered her mouth with her hands.

"Dana, she wants you to know that she is still around you and connected to you. She says you speak to her every day."

"Yes I do."

"You include her in your prayers don't you? She's says thank you. That the prayers are helping her to elevate and they bring her a lot of comfort."

"Thank you mom, I love you."

"She says she loves you too and that you have one brother correct? He is not doing as well her with her passing as you have."

"She's right. He is very depressed lately."

"Well, he has changed jobs she says recently. He is doing the same thing for a living but has changed locations of where he works."

"Oh my, yes. He will be so excited when I tell him this."

"Who is Sam? Is your brother Sam, because she is bringing up the name Sam."

Dana screams and makes me jump off my chair.

"Wow! Sam is going to die when I tell him this. This is just what he needs! He misses her so much. He lived with her and it was difficult for him to care for her in the condition she was in. He hated seeing her like that and carries a lot of guilt for not being more supportive. It was so hard for him to sit with her for any long period of time. He would get frustrated and leave the house."

"Rose says she understands he wasn't strong enough at the time to watch her deteriorate, but that she knows he's grown through the experience. She's saying he memorialized her in some way. He started either a foundation or some kind of organization she says."

"Yes," Dana said grinning from ear to ear. "We are very proud of what he's done. Sam created an awareness group in our hometown for victims of cancer. We're hoping it will provide resources to families as well as those who are assisting loved ones through treatment."

"She's saying it's time for her to go now. Keep praying for her she says and look for the signs she's giving you that she is around."

"Thank you so much."

Dana and I spoke after the reading of how her mother had come through with the obvious purpose of assisting her brother in his grieving process. Dana had waited for so long to make contact with her mother on the other side, and when that time was here, Dana became a messenger herself, with the mission of passing on to her brother that their mother could see what was happening in his life and what he had done for her in remembrance.

I recommended to Dana the book, *Hello From Heaven!*, by Bill & Judy Guggenheim. This book tells stories others have shared about their contact with loved ones in spirit and the many ways that after death communication can take place. I post this on my website and advise anyone wishing to learn the various ways spirit can come to us, to read it. When a spirit appears or shows itself to me, I usually see them in two ways. In perfect health, and then in the form of the illness or injuries they suffered while here on earth. Every spirit I have encountered though has always indicated to me that they no longer endure the limitations or wounds they may have endured while here. They are restored to perfect health and have overcome whatever restraints may have consumed them while in physical life.

Much has been written about After Death Communication and the ability of our loved ones who have passed on, to reach out to us and let us know they are near. In many instances...our loved ones who have crossed over may have *already* reached out to us. We just didn't know how to recognize their communication. They are in spirit now and must use other means by which to talk with us. They are trying to reach you because they love you. *The vital message here is that life never ends.* We are all souls...each one of us a unique energy pattern that lies beyond the form of physical matter and outside the limited forms of currently measurable energy. When you recognize their communication and presence, they have achieved their goal, which is to have us understand that they did not disappear when they died, but that they have only moved into another form. Learning to see and recognize these symbols, signs, and spirit language is the first step in accepting that our loved ones are still with us...just in spirit.

When faced with the task of mourning a treasured loved one, a profound measure of strength and will takes over. There are so many variables of situations involved when it comes to the death of an individual. What is instrumental in this huge sea of despair and confusion is that physical death is not the end. Your loved one's soul still permeates this earth and is around you in spirit. Many times I hear the phrase spoken, "dead is dead." It's interesting to note that in my line of work, I've often-time found that those individuals who were skeptical and possessed that analogy of death are the ones who as spirits, will try the hardest to communicate to their loved ones still in the physical world.

They have realized that life is eternal and goes on after we leave our physical bodies.

Energy can be neither created nor destroyed, only changed in form. We never really die. We receive a great number of signs, symbols, and validations from those who have crossed over into spirit. They want to communicate with us as much as we do with them. You only need open your mind to experience their existence again. Although you may no longer have the physical touch we as humans so desperately need to feel, you do have the ability to, in awareness, recognize when they are around you. The reassurance that they are still in our lives is paramount to the healing process of grief and bereavement. Once you can achieve a state of acceptance that they are no longer present in a physical sense, yet achieve the understanding that they *are here* in the spiritual sense and are safe and okay, you begin healing. Acknowledge their presence around you and recognize their existence. They will respond by letting you know in subtle ways they are there.

The bonds of love continue into infinity. It's those bonds of love that enable spirit to come through to us. Do not be discouraged if you have lost a loved one and feel they are not communicating with you. They truly are around you and watching over you. Many people have testified to the fact that it was some time, even years before they got a sign from their loved one that they were 'okay.' One life lesson we must all experience and learn is our everlasting quest to be in the likeness of God. There are many reasons why spirits contact us at particular times. As time passes you will see that we receive the messages we are meant to hear, and at the time we are meant to hear them. The old saying of "you may not always get what you want, but you get what you need" holds true. I encourage you to read, explore, speak to others who share the same grief and discover a new hope, information and a new realization that your loved ones beyond doubt are with you forever!

- Do all souls enjoy peace in the afterlife and is it a benevolent and joyous atmosphere always? –

If you've never seen the movie '*What Dreams May Come*' starring Robin Williams, rent it. This is the closest thing I know of, if you want a good visual, which accurately describes the symbolism and intricacies of the physical death and transformation process. If you are a literary person, pick up '*Life After Life* by Dr. Raymond Moody. *Life After Life* consists of case studies of near death experiences. Just as life is what you make of it here…so is death and the afterlife. Based on my experiences with clients, I have seen spirits come through and describe their surroundings established many times on their likes and dislikes here in the physical world. As an example, spirits will sometimes say they are still smoking or drinking, or they will show me a crystal house they are living in, and then I find out from the person I'm giving the reading to, that the spirit used to collect crystals. Spirits create the environment of their choosing founded on their comforts, what's familiar to them, and their well-being. Interestingly enough, this is the same with the actual crossing over process. If you are a lover of music, you will more than likely hear beautiful music when making the transition to the other side, before seeing the bright light. Someone however, who is not a lover of music or perhaps was emotionally traumatized when here, might hear a loud annoying buzzing sound instead. It's all relative.

- Are my loved ones okay? -

Yes! This is usually the first thing someone wants to know about their deceased loved one. They *are* in a better place and are in perfect, divine form. They will not possess any of the disabilities and handicaps they may have had in physical life.

- Are they happy and content? -

Most souls are blissful and jovial after they have crossed into spirit. They lose the physical limitations they had on earth, and are reunited with a divine spiritual awareness they had before being born. Not having those physical limitations allows them to reach us. Their spiritual intelligence allows them to assist and guide us. There are, however, other souls who may have been distressed while here on earth, frustrated with their own existence and lives. These souls, because of a plethora of reasons, were unable to work through certain issues, difficult lessons, or challenges that were bestowed on them. Whether their reason for crossing over was accidental death, suicide, or natural causes, these souls will continue to try to work through these issues and lessons with divine guidance and assistance in order to learn the lessons they were unable to while here on earth. Sometimes they may lend help to individuals here suffering the same afflictions as a way of learning and atonement. Good will always prevail, no matter what the essence or where it starts. God and his universe will perpetually produce 'virtuous good' eternally.

- Do they see me and when are they around me? -

Our loved ones are around constantly, especially when we have special moments in our lives, such as birthdays, celebrations, anniversaries and births. They are with us when we think of them. They are called to our presence when we need them. They witness all our triumphs and challenges. They are there sharing and enjoying the love and camaraderie of our families and friends just as they did when they were with us in the physical world.

- How do I recognize them? -

There are many signs and symbols that your loved ones are near. It could be the phone ringing, and when you answer it, there appears to be no one on the other end. The lights flickering or turning on or off by themselves. A radio that turns on or off mysteriously on its own. A butterfly that hangs around a window or door. Your pet staring intently at something, yet nothing appears to be there. Objects that come up missing, then found in a peculiar place. The feeling of a soft 'touch' somewhere on your body or a gentle tap on your shoulder, yet no one is there. You think of a loved one who is crossed, turn the radio or TV on and a specific song or show is playing which has significance related to your loved one. Road signs, street signs, book titles, billboards etc., that have hidden meanings at opportune times in your life. Witnessing an apparition or vision of them. There is an assortment of ways our relatives and friends use to communicate to us that they have not left us, and that they are still near and that they love us.

- Were they greeted by anyone when they crossed over? -

Our loved ones are always greeted by someone when they cross over in the spiritual realm. Most times they are greeted by a spouse or other family member or close friend who has gone on before them. You can be assured that they ARE NOT

ALONE. Aside from their family and friends who are already there, God is with them. He is a forgiving and ever-loving God, and no one will be left behind.

- Will I ever see them again? -

As the answer to the previous question stated...they are there to greet and assist us in crossing over, just as others were there to greet them.

- How do I let them know how I feel? -

You need only speak to them, in thought and prayer. They will hear you. And most times, will go as far as to give you signs that they heard your thoughts and prayers.

- How do I keep them in my life? -

Place pictures and acknowledgements of them around your home, work place etc. Recognize their birthdays, anniversaries and death dates in prayer and/or ceremony. Talk to them frequently and acknowledge their presence in your life. They will do the same, and give you signs that they are near you and watching over you.

- Do they care about family feuds or disputes? -

What may have been important to them in the physical world no longer holds the same luster or importance in the spiritual world, especially material possessions. They have no use for them. These possessions, most often, no longer matter to them. They only care about the joy and happiness these possessions may bring to you or those who still exist in the physical plane. Fights and disagreements are unnecessary in their eyes. Anything that comes in the way of love will be deemed unimportant and trivial. There is no room for envy, lust, or greed in the universal laws of spiritual existence. Love is eternal. Love is all that matters. God is love. God created us in his likeness. We too are love. What our loved ones see when they cross over is that LOVE is all that really matters.

~ *Understanding the Metaphysical* ~

The word metaphysical literally means that which is beyond the physical. In metaphysics when you examine the mind, you don't see it as being contained within the physical brain. You see the mind as energy, bringing a communicating interface between thought and feeling. For example, inspiration may start off from a feeling and then be transformed into a thought process which makes itself known in literature, science or the arts. The initial spark of the idea or impulse which actually produced that inspired mental process was a combination of impressions more related to feeling than thought. These feelings didn't originate in the physical brain. The physical brain just translated them into a recognizable form of intelligence.

I find it interesting to examine the states of consciousness which generate immense inspiration. Looking at it from the spiritual perspective, these states are created when the vibrations in your aura have been raised to a high level or frequency. In this state of consciousness, great inspiration will come to you in one form or another. Based on your work, what you are involved in at the time, and other factors, it will, for instance, come in the form of hearing wonderful sounds in your imagination, which then manifest into a great musical work. Monet, a great impressionist painter, saw magnificent relationships of color in his mind and was able to visualize this to such an extent that his expressions left us works of art in historic proportions. It might be an intuitive realization which leads to the invention of an important scientific work. A virtual uplifted state where a oneness with nature is felt and often experienced when engaging in heavy meditation. Religious writings also refer to elevated states of grace or higher consciousness. This is the state of consciousness that provides a medium affinity and connection with a person who is no longer living in a physical body but now inhabits a higher plane of existence and provides the opportunity for communication and a vehicle for messages to be passed from one plane to another. These inspirations result from elevated states of consciousness, which cause the physical brain to produce great thoughts. The brain is virtually a translating mechanism which helps to express the state of being of the individual.

- The Aura and Psychic Centers -

How many times have you walked into a room full of people and had an immediate sense of who you felt comfortable around and who you didn't? What makes you gravitate toward certain individuals rather than others? Your aura has a lot do with this. Imagine that your aura is a sensing machine. A well equipped device which sets off alarms any time its protective field is entered without permission. It will not only act as a protective alarm system, but also as a decipher machine. Breaking down and analyzing the energies of those in which it is exposed. Your aura is a wonderful mechanism which allows you, once you develop your abilities, to interpret and conclude information about not only other people near you, but also places, objects, and thoughts of events, reunions, etc. Picture your aura as the OZ in the '*Wizard of Oz*.' One central location for accessing all information that is thrust at it; your aura processes it, analyzes it and then reports.

Everything starts with the aura. It is the source of all mental and emotional functions within you. Auras are energy fields that surround the body like a huge egg. Most auras can eventually extend several feet around the body. It is believed that the more spiritually evolved a person is, the larger their aura. Everyone's aura consists of different layers. As you grow psychically you will be able to see these layers. Next to the physical body is the etheric double or sometimes called the etheric body. This is an extremely fine, almost invisible encasing that extends between a quarter to a half inch all around the body. It expands during sleep and contracts during the waking hours. Like a battery recharging itself overnight.

Your aura contains a multitude of different energies. These energies are received through your psychic centers known as chakras and travel throughout the aura in an intermingling network of channels known as nadis. Prana, or what's known as the life force in yogic philosophy, flows around our bodies through this network of nadis. There are 72,000 nadis inside the etheric body. The chakras are positioned on the principal nadi which runs alongside the spinal column. Everything we know and see is built from energy, including us. When trying to understand the psychic nature of the spiritual world, you must think in terms of energy and physics. Look at a nadis as an atom. These nadis are revolving, wheel-like circles of subtle energies that absorb higher energies and transform them into useable forms which are then utilized by the body. Our bodies contain currents of both positive and negative energies that come directly from our breath. For achieving the most advantageous energy balancing, the practice of Pranayama, or the science of correct breathing, is essential. When you meditate, which we'll get into in more detail in the next chapter, your breath work is key when trying to raise your level of vibrations, elevate to a higher level of consciousness, or any other type of psychic work. Being in good physical shape is a direct correlation to your ability to achieve quality results. Drinking, smoking, and other negative things we introduce into our body will inhibit your skills significantly.

There are seven major psychic centers or chakras in the body; the Root Chakra (located at the base of the spine), the Sacral Chakra, the Solar Chakra, the Heart Chakra, the Throat Chakra, the Christ Chakra or Third Eye and the Crown Chakra (positioned just above the head). These centers are in the aura and not in the physical body. They are also not necessarily positioned exactly opposite the relevant physical organ. For instance the heart center is in the center and not on the left-hand side of the body. The four bottom chakras are the quatern. They have a slower vibration rate than the three top chakras. The top three chakras are known as the triad. They are vibrating at a much higher rate than the lower four.

Whether or not we are acutely aware of the psychic centers and their function, they have purposeful effects on our daily lives. Along with working the internal transmission of energies, there is also a metaphysical relationship with our environment in which we live. Example; when you are on vacation and lying on the beach let's say, do you not feel the elation caused by being in an environment which is soothing, relaxing, and in nature? When on the other hand, riding on the crowded plane to get to that beach was an entirely different feeling. One of nervousness and anxiousness while waiting to get to your final destination. That is because on the plane, peoples auras where exchanging all types of information. Acting as a sponge they soak up everyone's negative thoughts, feelings, and energies and your aura was trying to process all that negativity. Consider that if you are in the company of a very vibrant person. Even if you do not exchange words with them, you will start to feel uplifted by their presence. If you are in the company of a depressed or pessimistic person, almost immediately you may start to feel negative and moody. This is the result of an interchange of psychic energies. This shows you the crucial importance in auras, especially in our psychic development. A developing psychic should strive to use all their psychic attributes in a positive, but always controlled fashion.

All the psychic centers have a vital function to perform. The more you use chakras (psychic centers) in a careful and balanced manner (incorporating all of them in your visualization and meditation exercises), the more you'll see the mind as a bridge between energies and thought processes. These energies move through your psychic centers into the aura.

For example the following is an exchange of letters between a woman named Denise and myself. She was in the process of developing her psychic senses. She had suffered a near death experience in a car accident which lead her to question her purpose here on earth and where her focus should be to make the most out of her life. I had told Denise to be prepared because once she openly requested help from spirit in strengthening her abilities, the 'floodgates would open.' Most often and rightfully so, once a person asks for guidance and assistance from above, spirit is quick to respond. God, your spirit guides and all other higher consciousness is waiting for you to make that request. As I've said many times, we are free will entities and must invite this into our lives. Once you do, I find they will acknowledge your request with great enthusiasm. Note what Denise is experiencing as she begins gaining psychic awareness. My responding letter follows hers.

"Dear Kathleen,

Please know how much I appreciated our phone conversation and that it meant so much to me. I felt an urge to share some of my thoughts and to inquire about some other (probably early stages of that flood gate you spoke of!) happenings I'm experiencing. I purchased the book *Life after Life* yesterday. It was very emotional for me because of the feeling and senses I had at the time when I was wandering in this gray, serene mist during my near death experience. I never have felt so protected in my whole life. I remembered how strongly I felt that I didn't want to come back, but to keep continuing through this place I was in. I never saw the bright light, not even a glimpse, but was folded among this an awesome comfort. I feel guilty now because I didn't have the slightest thought of my precious baby girl at the time, it's almost wrenching in a way to reveal this. Today cleaning the kitchen I was in my own little world, strongly going through little parts of my life and realizing now with significance what and why certain people have come into my life. These were parts that made you think twice, like back in the beginning of a relationship and I then, at that time, I knew for some reason I had to stay with that relationship. And now I know it was the right path for me to choose because I don't think I would have come to this awareness if I had gone in a different direction. This stuff is just coming to me all at once with an understanding that I never thought I would find on my own to a point. For the first time in my life this kind of feels really right to me, but during short periods I tend to hesitate or wonder about if I truly have this ability. I need an explanation about something I experienced last night. I had a weird dream that I can't fully remember and it seemed to be pretty intense. All I remember is shouting that I needed help. As I was coming out of the dream it seemed like I was going to verbalize my cry for help like talking in my sleep. I knew I was in my room and my husband was next to me, yet that was not a comfort. As I awoke I pulled the blanket over my head because I didn't want to look at anything. I was scared and overwhelmed but not remembering what the dream was to cause me to feel this way. It was something intense and weird that's all I remember from it. Does this mean anything? I tend to get very passionate and can really dig my heels into things I feel I have to pursue. It's the way I have

always been. I need to close this so it doesn't turn into chapters, I didn't think it would get this long, but there was a lot of stuff.
Sincerely,
Denise"

"Dear Denise:
I understand what you mean about the 'comfort' feeling in the grey mist and not wanting to come back. Please don't let that guilt stuff go too far because this is something that all of us will and do experience when in that state of the beyond. It is meant to feel that way. We are totally at peace. We have no more responsibilities other than to learn. We feel this way not because of a lack of care and love for our children or other relatives and friends, but because it is a higher consciousness that is so elating we know there is only one way to experience it and that is to stay there. Another key in the equation is when we are born into this earthly plane we forget what we've learned on the other side. We are born without this memory because if we remembered how we felt when in the spiritual world, we would never want to stay on the earthly plane! Not to mention, it would severely hamper are abilities to be objective and learn lessons. This is school. Earth is a learning ground. We all have many different and varied lessons to learn. With or without your assistance, your daughter has her own destiny and things to learn. As a higher consciousness (while experiencing your near death experience) you 'knew' that you did not need to be with her on the earthly plane for her to learn those lessons. She will undoubtedly embark on her own journey and learn in her own way at her own pace.

I understand completely what you mean about comprehending relationships and circumstances that made it possible for you to be where you are today. Denise, when you first invite spirit in to assist you with learning, many things take place. Imagine that your spirit guides are in that grey misty fog you described, yet they know where they are and can feel and sense where to go without hesitation and worry. You are the lighthouse. You flipped the switch on and now have alerted them to move in your direction. Remember I told of the importance of protection? You must continually protect yourself in white Godly light. You will be attracting your guides to help you but also other entities that sense you are putting your toes in the spiritual water and testing its temperature. They are hungry for an energy source and will tap into whatever is available to them. This is nothing to fear honestly and you are in total control of this always! Just consciously and continually, especially when meditating and before you go to sleep, imagine covering yourself in white light. This will work and be sufficient to stop anything negative. When you sleep, only your physical body sleeps. Your soul never goes to sleep so you are still "on" just not consciously. Keep a pad and pen by your bed and start practicing both when you drift off to sleep and also when you are awaking, speaking to your spirit guides and relatives in spirit. At both of those times, you have one foot in the spiritual world and one foot in the physical world. You will be successful in communication with spirit and can easily record whatever messages come through while it's still fresh in your mind.

Sincerely,

Kathleen"

Everyone is different, and each of us vibrates at a different rate of speed. The aura is a powerful thing and should be guarded as such. When you meditate, do it frequently with specific concentration on your chakras, cleansing them and removing any negativity from them. Always partake in a protection and grounding exercise when doing any type of metaphysical work.

When people first develop aura sight they usually see the etheric double first. The etheric double usually has a grayish tinge, and is constantly shimmering. You may also experience seeing changes of color in this etheric double. The constant movement inside the etheric double creates a wide variety of luminous colors that are constantly changing. Surrounding the etheric double is the aura proper. When the aura is first seen it appears to be white and almost cloud-like in appearance. Over time, as aura sight increases, colors can be seen more frequently. Every aura has a basic color that reveals important information about that person. A core-color if you will or what is called your ground color. This color shows the person's emotional, mental, and spiritual nature. With practice the characteristic of a person's ground color will tell you a great deal. Ideally, the ground color should be large in size, and rich in intensity. Once you have become used to seeing the ground color, you will gradually become aware of other colors that seem to exude outwards through the ground color. These colors indicate what the person enjoys doing. Usually, one or two colors will dominate, but a few people have a veritable rainbow of colors radiating out through the ground color. The happiest people are those whose colors combine. Below are some basic definitions of each ground color.

- Ground Colors -

RED
Leadership
A person with a strong ego and desire to achieve. These people frequently achieve positions of responsibility and leadership because they possess the necessary drive, energy, and charisma.

They are usually affectionate and warm-hearted. This is a powerful color to have.

ORANGE
Harmony/Cooperation
People who are naturally intuitive, tactful, and easy going. They are very gregarious, and often find themselves in positions where they have to smooth "troubled waters". They are usually thoughtful and down to earth, practical people.

YELLOW
Creativity /Mental Brilliance
People with a yellow ground color are enthusiastic, excitable and changeable. They are quick thinkers and enjoy entertaining and being entertained by others. They are social and excellent conversationalists. They are interested in learning, but can be lazy and skim over the surface of many subjects, rather than delve into one subject entirely.

GREEN
Healing
People who have this as their ground color are very peaceful and make natural healers. They may appear lazy and easy going, but can also be highly stubborn. They are cooperative, trustworthy and generous. The way to convince people with a green ground color of an idea is to make them believe that it was their own.

BLUE
Variety
Naturally positive and enthusiastic. Their auras are normally large and vibrant. They have a keen knack for always managing to climb out of trouble with apparent ease. They are sincere, honest and usually say what is on their mind.

INDIGO
Responsibility
It is usually difficult to determine this color as the ground color because it is so close to the color purple. People with it as their ground color usually end up in a humanitarian type of occupation. They enjoy helping and supporting others, and find their greatest happiness when surrounded by the people they love.

VIOLET
Spiritual/Intellectual
People with violet as their ground color develop spiritually all through their physical lives. Many people with violet try to fight their intuitive and spiritual natures. This creates an imbalance, and they will be aware that they are suffering some type of void in their lives. Once they start to learn and grow spiritually their auras also grow and become more vibrant.

SILVER
Idealism
It is rare to find silver as the ground color, though it is frequently seen as one of the other colors in the aura. People who silver as their ground color usually have a plethora of great ideas, yet most of them are not practical. These people often lack motivation.

GOLD
Unlimited
The most powerful ground color of all. The ability to handle large-scale projects and to achieve virtually anything. Charismatic, hard working, patient, goal-setting. Usually they achieve their greatest successes later in their lives.

PINK
Material/Success
This color appears as the ground color of determined, stubborn people. They set their sights high and then go after their goals with undaunted determination. They are often found in positions of power and responsibility. However, they are normally modest and down to earth people who enjoy the quieter side of life.

BRONZE
Humanitarianism
This color is rusty in appearance. People who have bronze as their ground color are caring, concerned, charitable individuals. They are sensitive and generous. They usually need to learn how to say "no" because others try to take advantage of them frequently.

WHITE
Illumination/Inspiration
White is rarely seen as the ground color. As all color comes from white, this is really just another name for light. People with it are normally lacking in ego and appear much more concerned with the well-being of others. These people are often highly intuitive and wise.

- *Radiating Colors* -

RED
People that like responsibility and enjoy making decisions. They seek power.

ORANGE
People who enjoy spending time with close friends and family. They are naturally intuitive.

YELLOW
People who enjoy new ideas. They like expressing themselves in various ways, such as singing, dancing, writing, especially talking!

GREEN
People who enjoy challenges and opportunities to prove themselves. They will work for however long it takes to get to their goals. They are natural healers.

BLUE
People who enjoy freedom and variety. They hate being limited. They enjoy travel and seeing new people and places.

INDIGO
People who enjoy helping others. They enjoy solving family problems and friends come to them often for solutions.

VIOLET
People who love to learn and grow in knowledge and wisdom. They often become involved in spiritual or metaphysical activities. They like to learn the hidden truths.

SILVER
People who enjoy coming up with great ideas. They can become totally lost inside their imagination, and are happiest in their own world.

GOLD
People who enjoy large-scale undertakings and big projects. They seek challenges that will test them and take them out of their comfort zones.

PINK
People who enjoy planning and dreaming about financial success. If they learn balance and harmony they can become astonishingly successful.

WHITE
People who are idealistic, and peace-loving. They enjoy supporting causes they believe in and look to create a better world for mankind.

- Aura Exercise -

This is a common exercise that is easy to do and I find it very productive in my classes and workshops. Ensure that the lighting in the room is soft. You do not want to do this under a bright light. Rather, sit so that any bright lights are behind you. You don't want lights shining in your eyes. Holding your fingers or hand over a light-colored surface (a sheet of white copy paper works well for most), stare at your fingers or hand yet notice the paper behind your hand at the same time, as if in your peripheral vision. While you are staring at your hand, it's this peripheral vision (looking at the object must at the same time focusing on the surface behind the object) where you will begin to see a silver shimmering color against your skin. Sometimes my students have witnessed ground colors rather than the silver shimmer and then some students have also seen both colors and a silver stream flowing against their skin. Any one of these combinations can be seen when first learning to read and see auras. Once you are able to see it, you'll find you are able to see these threads of energy at any time, under any circumstances. Please practice over and over. As with any skill...the more you practice the better you will become. It took me several tries before I could see my aura. Keep in mind that you have many psychic gifts. No one person is going to be great at everything. I find that out of the five psychic senses most people are good at three and okay at the other two. Just as everyone can paint, not everyone is a Monet. Go easy on yourself, recognize your strengths and then utilize the sense that work best for you. You want to always be open to all five senses, but concentrate on what works best for you. Your guides know what your strengths are and will be proficient in getting the messages to you using whatever methods necessary based on the particular message they need to convey. Always trust the information you receive. Believe in your guide's ability to assist you and you will be successful in seeing or sensing auras, using your psychic senses and connecting with spirit.

~ *Meditation and Raising Vibrations* ~

- *Meditation* -

Meditation is a purposely induced state where the physical body and conscious mind are bypassed temporarily so the inner self comes into focus. Through a series of mental and visualization exercises the body is rested, and at the same time, the mind emptied of any random thoughts enabling a connection between conscious and subconscious to take place. It is at this point that a state of pure heightened awareness without thought is attained. Practice will make it easier for the psychic to 'drop into' the level where all psychic activity takes place.

You will notice some enhanced benefits gained from ritualistic meditation. A healthier immune system and the ability to withstand stress and remain calm naturally are often experienced as a bonus. A proper balanced diet, low in caffeine, sugar, and other items that rob our body of nutrients plays an important part in your ability to do psychic work. Please try to not eat any heavy meals for at least two hours prior to meditating or doing any medium work. If your body is trying to digest a heavy meal, it is undermining the focus that you will be trying to place on it during meditation.

- *Meditation / When and Where* -

The best time to meditate is a time when you know you will not be interrupted. Some say the shower is a great place to meditate because the water is soothing and you are seldom interrupted there. I find that if you are a beginner, it's best to meditate sitting upright. You can meditate lying down or at night also, but sometimes the work and stress of the day may cause you to fall asleep. Find a place where you won't be disturbed by noises, telephones, or other people barging in on you. Sit upright either on the floor or in a straight back chair with a cushion so you are comfortable.

The object of the process is two-fold; to relax the body and to subdue the thoughts that continuously run through our mind. You do this by occupying the mind with the process of relaxing the body. As the body relaxes, so does the mind. Our soul never sleeps, so you can achieve states of relatively long periods where the mind is silent, yet is receiving messages. During any mediumship exercise you should always focus on two things. One is protection, the other is grounding yourself. Without fulfilling these two tasks you will run the risk of being an open conduit for energies and entities. They will deplete your positive energy which enables them to gain strength, as well as drain you of significant energy necessary for your physical body to operate normally.

When first learning to develop my channeling abilities I once attended a Circle of Light (a séance for you newbies) where the medium leading the group failed to instruct us on protection and grounding. The evening, I thought at the time, went very well. Just about everyone in the room received messages from those departed and she had brought through several people for me. In gathering our energies at the beginning of the session, I felt my physical body, my upper torso, start to spin in a clockwise direction. At first I thought; "Wow, this is cool. I'm really getting into this here." As the night went on and we finished the session I didn't have any other physical sensations but enjoyed watching the medium deliver the messages. As my husband and I (he's good about coming along for the ride) left the circle, we decided to stop at a local restaurant and grab a bite to eat before heading home. In the ten minutes it took to get to the car, I started experiencing a nauseous feeling in the pit of my stomach. By the time we reached the restaurant, fifteen minutes later I was explaining to Lou that I was not feeling well at all and very woozy. We had already ordered our food when I asked him if he was experiencing anything similar. He said he felt fine and that maybe I was coming down with a bug of some kind. We finished dinner quickly and on the drive home I laid in the reclined front seat.

We lived near the restaurant so by the time we got home, only forty-five minutes had passed since we had originally left the bookstore where we had attended the Circle of Light. By this time, I was just barely able to crawl upstairs and make it to my bed. I remember my chest feeling as if there were heavy bricks on it, like when you're coming down with bronchitis. It felt like the room was spinning and I prayed that I would be able to go to sleep quickly. When I awoke in the morning I was still a little groggy, and my chest muscles were somewhat sore, (like when you're up all night with a bad cough). I was now thankful that I was able to walk around and had a little energy. Knowing that what had happened to me was directly related to the previous night's events and not a virus, I called the aid of a good psychic for her opinion of what had happened to me and how I would go about preventing this discomfort in the future. My good friend Leona, is a Reiki Master and has been a practicing psychic for several decades. In other words, she knows her stuff, and I trust her opinion. She confirmed what I had suspected. She immediately asked what techniques were used in protecting me before beginning the ceremony. When I answered, "There were none," she told me that I should develop my own ways of protection before I practice any type of mediumship. That I was an open instrument used by spirits that night so they could communicate with the rest of the room. She informed me I was probably not the only person in the room to experience the discomfort. The point to this story is that spirits, however innocent they may be, must gain their energy from somewhere. Everything you do in psychic work you are totally in control of, if you adhere to guidelines and rules. Psychic work is a science just like any other. Follow some basic principles and you will be successful as a psychic and medium. When you protect yourself in white light, you are asking God, your Maker, or the supreme being of your choice to protect you against any negative, foreign or obtrusive forces. An affirmation also said before each meditation process is tone setting and will become buried in your subconscious as another positive shield. I have written below the affirmation I use before channeling, but create one of your own that is both personal and exudes your spiritual awareness.

My inner wisdom grows stronger and clearer,
every day in every way.
I am a clear channel of love and light;
I am well guided both day and night.
I hereby release any previous distrust of
my own judgment and decisions;
I now trust my higher self to guide me well.
I open mind and heart and now perceive
all higher guidance that I receive.
I release former fears and send them away.
I am calm, I am still, my heart and life, God-Light does fill.
Everything I am and do is through God.

- Meditation / The Process -

Sit in your selected place and relax yourself. Take a few deep breaths paying deliberate attention to the sound of the air as it enters and exits. Imagine as you draw deep breathe into your lungs, that this breathe is a white-golden color. See the white-golden air filling your lungs, traveling through your bloodstream and reaching your entire body. As you exhale this breath, imagine this exiting your body as gray and black air. You are breathing in the positive white-golden Godly light and exhaling all the negatives and impurities of your mind and body. As you inhale and exhale, practice counting mentally to five. This will ensure you're taking in deep relaxing breaths. After much practice you will no longer need to count to reach a rhythmic state of breathing. Focus your mind on your body and begin instructing it to relax. Beginning at the top of your head, instruct the muscles to relax, and then actually feel these muscles relax. Move on to the face and neck muscles, focusing your mind on instructing your body to relax these muscles and then actually feeling the muscles relax before you go on. Continue doing this until you have reached your toes. You should then be aware of the relaxed state your body is in. If at any time your mind drifts onto something else, just return it back to the task of relaxing your body parts. Don't fight or struggle against these thought intrusions, just let them go peacefully away, and continue the process.

Next, imagine a huge ball of white-golden light at your feet. This ball of heavenly light is getter larger and larger. As it rests on your feet you start to sense its warming capabilities. Your feet and toes are getting warmer and warmer. See this ball of light now begin to travel up your calves and shins. You feel the warm peaceful sensation as this Godly light wraps your body in its protection. Protecting you from any harm or evil, this light continues traveling up across your knees, and now to your thighs, encasing you in immense bright white-golden protective light. This ball of light is now encasing your pelvis area, feel it as it crosses over your chakras. Sense your chakras tingling and soaking up this light. The light now passes over your stomach, back, chest, neck, face, and out through the top of your head and falls all over you to surround your entire body. You are now sitting in a protected and guarded ball of white-golden light. Imagine this light now stretching out over the room where you sit, now the entire house or building. The light continues to encircle the whole city, then the state, then the earth. You feel your connection to the earth and your place in the universe.

Now begin to relax your mind. This next part helps to train your mind to focus. You are about to create your "Psychic Private Place." This is a place where no one can enter but you. Only you have the key to get in this private place. You are never to bring anyone else to your private place. This is where you will be met by your spirit guides, and angels. Do not expect to see them right away, as you are still building and creating this private place. Your guides and angels will reveal themselves to you when they know you are psychically ready to meet them. I have had students who have met their guides in the beginning stages of development, but this is rare. Be open to all possibilities. If in fact it is a guide with whom you are communicating, they will let you know in various ways the experience is in fact real. Although your spirit guide is mentioned in this exercise, you can visualize a silhouette until your guide reveals him or herself. You can create this private place any way you desire but the following is an example of what you might construct when building your journey to your psychic room or psychic private place.

Imagine yourself stepping into a wonderful peaceful garden. This garden is full of the most beautiful trees and soft grass you have ever seen. The colors of green are luminous and brighter than any of the greens you have seen before. You spot birds flying amongst the trees and hear them chirping merrily. See a cool white stone path before you that winds out into the distance deeper and deeper into your garden. As you begin slowly walking along the path, you feel the warm soft breeze blowing over your skin, making your skin feel as if God is caressing your body. You feel his warm inviting love, and are anxious to continue your journey. You feel totally at peace and know that you have nothing to fear. God is there, he is protecting you, and you are in total control of your surroundings. Look up to the sky above you and see the magnificent hues of blues, greens, yellows, oranges, reds, and violets, all iridescent colors floating gently in the sky with white billowy clouds. These are all of God's colors. Like a kaleidoscope, its beauty is glorious and brilliant. You now see squirrels, chipmunks, rabbits, and other small creatures playfully jumping in the garden as you continue down your stone path. The sounds of a babbling brook are heard. You can hear the water hitting the rocks in the bed of the river and the cool water travels at a high rate of speed downstream. As the path winds around to the right you now see the stream come into view. The rushing water looks cool and inviting. Now you see a bridge. You intuitively know that this is no ordinary bridge. This bridge will lead you to another more secluded area of your garden. You step onto the bridge and let your hand gently slide on the railing as you cross over to the other side. You notice that the stone path is now gone and your feet step off of the bridge onto a smooth velvety cushion of grass. Across this prairie of green velvet, you notice a sheer purple veil suspended in the air. This purple veil is the only thing you see in this valley of green. Although you are not moving, you begin to feel the white-golden light that surrounds you start to spin in a clockwise direction. You watch as this light commences to spin faster and faster. A feeling of warmness comes over you and you can feel your energy level rising rapidly. You feel the vibrations coming from within your deepest recesses and chakras begin to increase their speed. You feel your whole body vibrating at a tremendous rate and it feels marvelous, exciting, and exhilarating! You now start to walk over to this veil and when you come up to it, you see a figure of someone standing on the other side. There is no fear and you are not afraid, but instead feel an immediate pull to this individual. As if you and they were magnets. This veil is a door, the door to your psychic room. Your spirit guide is here to take your hand and lead you across this veil into the psychic realm. You reach out your hand and take one side of the veil and pull it back gently. With your other hand, you extend it to take the hand being offered you by your spirit guide.

After assisting you across, he/she no longer needs to hold your hand, but will stay with you until you feel comfortable with your surroundings. As you look around, practice asking your guide mentally, questions such as…

- What's your name?
- What purpose do you serve in my life?
- What is it that I need to learn?
- Are there particular colors, sounds, or fragrances that will draw you closer?
- Is there anything specific that I need to know at the moment?
- How can I help in building our relationship?
- Are there any messages that you have for me?
- Are you male or female?
- Designate the spot where you wish your spirit guide to touch you on your body and tell him/her. Let them know you wish to use this so you know when they are around you. It will help you to distinguish your guide from other spirits which may be there.

Don't force anything! Just allow yourself to receive and be open to whatever messages come through. While in your psychic room, you should develop tools by which your angels, and spirit guides can speak to you. For instance, you might picture a monitor or screen on which they can write messages, numbers, dates, names, etc. Build and design this room to your own satisfaction and tastes. You should feel comfortable and completely at ease here. Maybe a tree in one corner, a favorite couch in the other, or add specific candles or fragrances.

When you are ready to end your visit here, it is very important that you ground yourself properly when leaving and returning to the physical realm. Whatever your visualization is (we're using a garden in this one), make sure you exit the same way you entered. That is grounding. I will walk you through this in a moment. As I stated before, remember that you are an open conduit when performing this type of mental and spiritual exercise, in connecting the spiritual realm with the physical realm. Protecting yourself as you leave from harmful energies is vital to guard against physical sickness and weaknesses in your aura. As you say goodbye to your angels and guides, be sure to thank them, and God, for all the assistance they provided you. Tell them you look forward to seeing and meeting with them again real soon. As you approach the door (or veil) in your room and step through it, be sure to leave through your garden the same way you entered. Cross over the plush field and feel the soft green grass under your feet. You feel your vibrations slowing slightly as you begin to see your bridge appear in the distance. You walk up to the bridge and cross over it, again caressing your hand along the rail as you go over. Step onto the stone path which will eventually lead you back to the entrance. You once again spot the pebbled brook beside the path and see the water swiftly hitting the rocks. As you continue down your stone path you see the squirrels, chipmunks, rabbits, and other small creatures playing in the garden. You look above you and again see the magnificent hues of blues, greens, yellows, oranges, reds, and violets, all iridescent colors floating gently in the sky with white billowy clouds. As you near the front of your garden you see a white stone bench. Sit on your bench and feel God's white light around you, protecting you against the outside forces of the world.

Imagine that God's light will continue to guard and protect you forever and ever. You can now leave your garden. Slowly open your eyes and begin to move your fingers and toes. Touch something around you to ground yourself again, such as the chair, a desk, etc.

The purpose of this exercise to occupy your mind with the process of meditation, leaving no room for extraneous thoughts to enter. As you practice meditation you'll find that it gets easier to avoid the thoughts that are in your mind. Focus decreases the impact of random thoughts and allows you to drift into the state of psychic focus much easier. You will be able to go to your psychic place at will, with your eyes open, and be moving freely about…even carrying on multiple conversations with others while communicating with your angels and guides. That is when you will be able to use a subconscious 'trigger' to drop into an 'on' and 'off' position quickly. The more frequently and diligently you meditate (remember to do it at the same time each day if possible), the more you will increase your psychic strengths. When first developing your meditation and visualization skills, be sure to keep a tablet or paper of some kind close by to write down any and all experiences you encounter. The smallest and seemingly insignificant symbols, images, or pieces of information received during these exercises will be pieces of a puzzle that your guides assist you in putting together, so you can one day 'see the big picture.' You will find these notes extremely valuable to your development process.

~ *The Five Psychic Senses* ~

Our sensing ability both physically and especially psychically is quite remarkable. If you learn to trust the information you feel, see, hear, dream, taste and smell you will make tremendous strides in gaining knowledge and understanding in both the physical and spiritual worlds. We use all of our various senses every day. I received a letter from a guy named Dan who was experiencing precognitive dreams. At the onset he would dismiss them as coincidences. As his dreams became more frequent, the accuracy was too telling of something other than just dreams at work. This is what Dan wrote;

"I have dreams fairly often and in them there are complete strangers. People I have never met or seen before. Then in the near future, either a couple days or sometimes a few weeks, I will meet a person that looks exactly like the person in my dream. Probably my first and most moving experience with this was about 10 years ago when I dreamed I was married to this certain girl. Then she shows up at my school the very next Monday having moved from another state! I had an infatuation with her for the longest time after that."

As I said in Chapter 12, you do have many out of body experiences and partake in astral travel unknowingly. We meet up with other souls both living and deceased for many reasons. Some to work out unfinished karmic business, some to assist each other at becoming more skilled in a specific task. The list is endless. Precognition means you are getting the information before it happens, knowledge of a future event or situation through extrasensory means. Consider that your spirit guides are also helping you to have these precognitive dreams and have several motives. One motive is so that you learn to trust information you're given from them, another is so they have the ability to get your attention and are hoping you will search for ways to develop your psychic skills in an effort for you to better understand them and the channel of communication they are building with you. You have specific items to accomplish on your spiritual checklist in this lifetime.

Not everyone has the luxury of experiencing precognitive dreams. Each one of us graduates to a new level after completing our education here. Based on what you've learned, some may excel to the head of the class, while others may be in the remedial group. There is really no right or wrong speed at which to grow. Each life time will provide you with answers and wisdom to elevate you to the next level. I am of the opinion that those of you who do have precognitive dreams, experience them because your soul has learned many lessons and is vibrating at a higher level.

Recognizing when spirit is working with you through your dreams is a way of opening a new channel by which you can then receive other messages as in the case with Theresa. She shared with me her discoveries of after death communication which started through dreams and spilled over into her every day life. Theresa wrote;

"One of the hardest things about losing a loved one is the not knowing what really happens when you die. Society tends to discourage us from acknowledging those precious communications from beyond and we shut down. I lost a very dear love recently. I dream of him often. Some dreams are very comforting and others seem to be explaining or even apologizing for things that had happened when he was here. When I have these dreams I remember them very well, they stick with me throughout the day. Sometimes, I wake feeling as if I was actually with him (those are the best ones!!!). Another thing that seems to be communication comes through the radio. My loved one was very musical so this makes perfect sense to me. There have been times where I was asking him a particular question about how he died and at that moment a song would come on the radio that seemed to be answering the question. I often talk with him either out loud or in my head and I seem to hear him responding to me in my head. Actually, just today I was making tuna fish salad and I heard his voice in my head telling me how much he liked the way I made it, even offering a critique on the one I was making at the time. Imagine how good it makes me feel to know these experiences are not signs of mental illness on my part, but actual conversations."

A 'visit' from a loved one who has passed can be quite common. Most of us will toss these dreams off as just that, dreams. Our subconscious is what communicates to spirit; our conscious self is only a facilitator of the information and communication taking place. Let's face it, most people are not psychic mediums with the ability to tap into the other side whenever they desire to hear from uncle Mike. However, the spirits of our loved ones know that they can reach into our subconscious to make that connection. So they will visit us in dreams when our consciousness is out of the equation. Pay attention to your dreams and learn to record the information you receive from your guides and spirit both as you sleep, and when you drift off or awake from the sleep process. Keep a pad and pen or pencil next to where you sleep. Track and record what you feel, hear, sense, taste, smell, and see in those times. If you are asking your God, spirit guides and loved ones for guidance in understanding the language of spirit they will be there to help and assist in your learning. They are anxious for you to build that bridge between your world and theirs. The more you record, the more you will begin to see and comprehend a message and fluidity of the information they are delivering you. Don't worry you do not have to be Sigmund Freud, or a scholar of psychoanalysis to determine what it is that you are supposed to do, or what it is they are trying to tell you. Let your intuition and what most of us refer to as our gut instinct, be your guide on how you process the information. I promise you, spirit will provide the answers and position people and places in your path to direct you in the right direction. Not to say that you believe everything that you see and hear, be skeptical. Ask questions both of spirit, and also of the other resources you tap into such as books, recordings, classes and the like, while continuing to develop your psychic senses. I was careful to always check references on other professionals in the psychic field when doing any type of study or research. I made sure that they had strong, successful reputations and found the mentors I needed to help me hone in on my skills. I do believe that spirit was there guiding me. In a literal sense, I was led by spirit when looking for particular manuals and books in the metaphysical genre. I was once walking in a Half Price Books store searching for a book that would assist me in strengthening my communication with spirit guides. As I perused the shelves, one lone book was facing outward with the cover staring directly at me. Someone had placed this book back on the shelves carelessly, probably in a hurry. There it was bigger than life, *"How to Meet and Work with Your Spirit Guides"* by Ted Andrews! Well I did take that as a sign, and bought the book. It was helpful, and once again, I thanked my Guides for being so courteous and timely with their assistance.

Back to visits...unfortunately not everyone is guaranteed a visit. But also don't think that just because your loved one hasn't reached out to you in a dream that it means they do not want to speak with you. They also are restricted to certain degrees concerning their level of ability to make that connection, whether it is karmically correct to make an appearance at that time based on your progress in spiritual awareness, and so forth. There are a lot of parameters in the spiritual world. I'm sure we have yet to learn what dictates who gets visits and who doesn't. For some of us lucky ones, a visit is understood and recognized right away. Visits by our loved ones will be defined in your dream because of the clarity in which you see, feel, and remember their presence. Visit can be long or short and varying or repetitious; it's a very personal and individual experience for everyone. The following is a letter I received from Helen who enjoyed more than one visit from her sister Mary.

"My deceased loved ones come to me in my dreams, or am I dreaming?!! My Aunt Ruth passed on when I was twelve years old. I have not thought of her at all. She appeared to me last night. I asked who she was and she told me, I am your Aunt Ruth. Over the tears I felt myself floating towards the song Ava Maria, where someone was singing. I felt so peaceful drifting closer and closer to the song that when I awoke. I immediately tried to go back to sleep. I wanted more of the peace I had experienced and wanted to eventually get to where the song was coming from. I had even lain down to recapture it all. My sister Mary visited me one night in a dream. She expired from breast cancer twenty-one years ago. In this dream we sat out on the patio and talked for awhile. Mary called me by my nick name, "Helba," she had given me. Then she said to me, "well Helba, we better go in now because I know you are afraid to stay out past dark." As we walked into her home, immediately my eyes saw a large Bible she had lying on her bed. Another night Mary came to me and told me where the torch light was to keep the bugs away before we were going to have a picnic. The next day I asked my brother-in-law if there was a torch light behind the house where Mary had described and he said, yes! We went to the back yard and there it was. I also dreamed one night that I passed on and I was levitating above all my loved ones. I have had many more unusual happenings. I am a true believer in everlasting life."

Remember that you are a multi-faceted entity and soul. You possess a conscious mind, a physical body, a subconscious mind, and a spiritual body. Always think in those terms, and inevitably you will see with different eyes and hear with different ears. When learning the language of spirit, incorporate all of your senses in the process. As with any skill, practice makes perfect, so practice over and over again until you develop a recognizable and fluid conversation style with the spirit realm. You can practice with friends and family members, but as I said before, practicing with strangers works best. You are operating from a clean slate. You have no preconceived notions, expectations, or knowledge of these individuals or their families that would interfere with trusting the information you're given by the spirit. There is no second-guessing involved in the process. Just trust and pass on all the information you are given. If you come to a point in the reading where you are unsure what the symbols mean, simply ask spirit to give you more. They will. Even if you are not interested in becoming a practicing psychic but rather only want to learn the language of spirit to communicate with your loved ones, there is an important lesson learned when doing readings for others. My advice is, by reading for others you will accurately determine what that spirit language is. How it sounds and what it feels like. You will build confidence in knowing how to recognize and communicate with spirit. There are five psychic senses just as there are five physical senses. I have written a description of each sense.

Clairvoyance is the ability to interpret objects, symbols and scenes from the spirit in the form of sight. These images can be both literal and symbolic. Do an exercise with me. Keeping your eyes open, imagine what your vehicle looks like. Now picture the Empire State building, and then see your bed. Now envision what your mother looks like. What you pictured in your mind for each one of those examples, is what clairvoyance is. When spirit shows me a picture, I see it just as you saw your bed. What we assume many times are random images we think of 'out of the blue' are really messages from spirit. If we treat them as communication from spirit, you will see they are creating a message for you, one picture at a time! Clairvoyance is also a way for spirits to convey what they looked like when in their physical bodies. When I do a reading, the spirit either shows me themselves or someone who looks like them, sometimes a character from a television show, like Raymond from *Everybody Loves Raymond* in order to let me know how they looked, or what their personality is like. But sometimes they may show me Raymond because they were a big fan of the TV show, or the name, Raymond itself, and the person I am reading for will instantly recognize this.

Clairaudience is your ability to hear sounds and voices coming from spirit. Sometimes the voices are male or female, but most often it is in your own voice that you hear spirit speaking. So how do you differentiate between your voice and those coming from the spirit world? Mostly, what I hear are messages in my own mind's voice. Visualize you are reading a book and at the same time thinking, did I turn off the coffee? That is your mind's voice. Trust what you hear, especially after asking spirit a question. The first response you hear is always the right one.

Clairsentience is probably the most common of all the five psychic senses. Most people refer to this as your 'gut feeling' or 'gut instinct.' Even auras can felt rather than seen when interpreting colors. You use clairsentience all day long. When you enter a room full of people, you automatically feel what side of the room you would rather be on. Or how about when you are first introduced to someone and you get a distinct impression of them right away? Why is it that even when we don't know someone, and upon first meeting them, we may feel like we have known them for years and have a great connection with them? And others we would rather not have to endure a second encounter. It's our subconscious using our clairsentience, our psychic feelers, determining whether it's safe to go in the water or not. Clairsentience also allows you to have the ability to 'feel what the spirit is feeling' either right now or before they crossed over. This is also how spirits convey emotions or physical discomfort and pain they may have experience when in physical form. When I am able to convey messages of health problems, I often feel physically what parts of the spirit's physical body had the health issue. If they had chronic arthritis I might feel pains in my joints. Or if they had emphysema, I might feel tightness in my throat or chest. Spirits cannot take over your physical or mental state without your permission. Please understand that you are in control at all times and can stop these sensations at any moment. Spiritual law dictates that if a spirit is bothersome and you ask them to leave, they will always leave. If you've heard of people being influenced by negative spirits, you will find that they had other issues as well such as; drug use, drinking, and an unhealthy lifestyle perhaps or were mentally or emotionally unstable. Bad spirits can only visit you if you ask them to. They must be invited in. And likewise, when asked to leave, they must leave. Always surround yourself with white light, do this work in divine thought, and you never have to worry.

Clairalience is the ability to receive smells psychically. You'll find that you will smell various scents and fragrances related to the person crossed over such as smoke for instance is they were a smoker or possibly died in a fire. Specific perfumes they wore are common, as well as spices they used and favorite fragrances they enjoyed. These are all ways that spirit can communicate a message. My spirit guide told me early on in my development that lavender was a scent that would draw him closer to me. I now burn lavender candles during most of my readings.

Clairhambience is being able to get tastes in a reading. During a session, I began to taste the tartness of an orange and my mouth started watering. Although I wasn't 'seeing' the images of oranges I felt like I had a huge wedge of an orange in my mouth. When I explained to the woman I was reading for what I was experiencing and asked if there was importance regarding oranges, she about fell over! This spirit evidently loved orange juice and made a habit of drinking a glass every day when he was alive. To her, this seemingly small piece of information was a huge validation for her that she was indeed hearing from her husband. Clairhambience is one more way which spirit uses to get their message across. They will utilize any of or all of the five psychic senses to make that happen.

You are receiving messages daily, you may just not know it. Watch for cold spots in your house. Have you ever felt spider webs around your face yet you couldn't see it and were walking through your kitchen perhaps (somewhere where it's unlikely to run into a web)? Notice if lights flicker on and off. Spirits also like to use computers, clocks, radios, and the telephone. Ever get a phone call yet no on was on the other line? Computers, clocks and radios can go on or off by themselves. What about your dog or cat that is nervous for no apparent reason and is staring at something, yet nothing is there? Spirits will use all sorts of signs to let us know they are around us.

Sometimes I'm asked why the messages received aren't more insightful or philosophical. My belief is messages from spirit that validate their existence, is indeed profound. I feel that no matter what message comes through, maybe one word or maybe an hour long session of information, the amount of energy that spirits have to expend to reach us is enormous. These validations can hopefully help us heal and possibly bring us closure in knowing that the bonds of love between us and our loved ones are there forever. We should be thankful and acknowledge their existence and the messages we receive.

While carrying out readings for a group one evening I was told of a fascinating story I'll share with you. A woman named Adel was joyfully planning her wedding and as the big day drew near, it came time to have her bachelorette party. Her sister Angie was her maid of honor and had the responsibility of putting the affair together. Angie's husband, Stan, had been battling depression for some time and seemed lately to be more melancholy than ever. Adel knowing this, had mentioned to her sister that it wasn't necessary to have a bachelorette party, trying to remove some of the stress Angie was enduring. Angie, being a good sister, swore that it was no trouble and that she was moving ahead with her plans. The party would be held at Adel's house.

The night of the party, the girls were having a great time, playing games, eating hors d'oeuvres and enjoying each other's company. Adel heard the phone ring in the next room and got up to answer it. When she picked up the phone there was no one on the line. She said hello repeatedly and got no response, so she hung up. As she began walking back to the living room, as she passed her patio door, she noticed her brother-in-law, Stan. She opened the door with a smile and asked if he wanted to come in. He said no, but would she mind sitting on the patio with him for a few moments because he had something he wanted to tell her. He seemed very calm and pleasant and knowing the state he'd been in lately, she obliged. They sat together and Stan told her how much he loved her and that he was very sorry if his depressive state had put a damper on her wedding plans. He said he was feeling much better and that he would not let his depression ruin her impending marriage date. She told him that it was okay, and that she just wanted him to be alright and not to worry. They then stood up, embraced, and said good-bye. Stan left through the side yard the same way he had entered. When Adel went back into the house, she immediately went to her sister and told Angie that Stan had come by and that he was leaving if she wanted to say good-bye to him on the driveway. When Angie walked outside Stan was already gone.

Later that night Adel got a disturbing call from her sister. When Angie arrived home, Stan was dead. He had ended his life. The coroner, when examining the body, ruled the time of death at the same time he had appeared to Adel on her patio. Adel realized that she had experienced a 'visit.' That Stan had come to say good-bye one last time and asked for forgiveness for all the pain he'd caused while dealing with his illness.

Sometimes language of spirit is very direct, and other times it's vague. Because we have many different senses by which we receive and process information, our loved ones will use whichever of those senses will work best at getting their message to you. In the case of Denise, she experienced 'visits' also from a dear friend who had passed. These visits provided healing and a knowing that her friend was not dead, but was still very much alive in spirit and around her. Our loved ones do want to communicate with us and if we consider being open to it, they are sure to make that connection.

Denise was accepting of the connections from others who had passed. When Bob first appeared to her it was only one week after his death. Her husband and Bob were best friends. Denise described their relationship saying they had always felt like the brothers neither of them had. She was close with Bob's wife as well and the four of them spent a lot of time together on family outings with their respective children. One morning as Denise awoke and lay in bed waiting for the alarm to go off, Bob appeared to her. He was standing at her bedside. Bob had been well over six feet tall and appeared as such that day. He was in full view, towering over her as Denise stared at him for fifteen seconds or so. Shocked, she closed her eyes thinking 'here I go again.' This was not Denise's first encounter with an apparition, but was astonished that Bob had come to see her. With his death so new, she was understandably very emotional. Denise opened her eyes slowly and watched as Bob gradually faded away. A little shaken, she wondered what his visit was supposed to mean. Was she supposed to say something? He didn't. Was she to give a message of some kind to his wife? Why did he come to her? The other after death communication experiences Denise had, were different. They started with someone was trying to come through, but she hadn't seen an actual form, just a fuzzy, swirling figure of a fog like substance which disappeared as soon as she noticed it. Then her father-in-law appeared briefly a month after his passing. After a few seconds he disappeared. Those two appearances took place within two months of each other. Denise began to question why all of this was happening to her.

I explained to Denise that I believe it is spirit's goal, whether it is our guides or loved ones coming through, that we learn to acknowledge and accept that there is more than what we physically see and understand. There is another whole dimension of life force happening simultaneously, and we can be a part of that dimension if we learn a few basic principles. Our lives become more clear, defined and rooted in a fundamental philosophy of helping and loving one another. Sometimes using others to pass on messages of healing is what is needed at that particular time. Denise friend Judy, wife of the Bob, may not have been emotionally prepared for such a shock to see her deceased husband standing next to her so soon after his physical death. The sever and numbing separation anxiety experienced when you have lost someone close to you, can and is sometimes devastating. Seeing a vision or apparition of her husband might have sent Judy into an even deeper and more traumatic depression. Bob knew that the best course of action was to visit Denise, someone who would recognize and interpret his visit and then gently pass the experience on to his widow at a time when she could absorb the occurrence in the right manner.

I would like to share another story of spirit communication with you. Rick, who lives in San Gabriel, California, shared his experiences with me which took place shortly after his wife, Marlene of twenty seven years passed after a two year battle of breast cancer. While facing the struggle of the diagnosis, Rick was told that Marlene had possibly four years to live. Unfortunately her illness took in just two. Rick was left with the task of raising their three sons, ages twenty-one, seventeen and nine. Marlene was a large supporter of spiritual communication. She had read books about reaching the other side and how the earthly and spiritual worlds blend as one universe. Marlene, being a strong believer in this process, had briefly spoken about it with Rick but unfortunately didn't have the opportunity to discuss it in detail. Rick did however share with her he felt spirit communication was possible. She asked of Rick, if after she passed, would he please speak to her every evening. He says he does regularly and asks her to make her presence known to him. Not so much to tell him that she is okay, his strong Christian faith tells him that she is, but to confirm to Rick that they will be together again. What was most important for Rick was to know that he would one day be reunited with the wife that he loved so dearly.

Five minutes before Rick and his children were to leave for Marlene's funeral service he noticed the light in her curio cabinet wouldn't stay on. There had never been a problem with the light fixture in the cabinet, yet when he turned it on, it would go off. Rick felt (as I do too) it was Marlene's way of getting his attention, letting him know she was around them that day. He also experienced another sign from Marlene on the day he was en route to witness the placement of her headstone. After exiting the mortuary office and receiving instruction to follow the mortuary worker to the gravesite, he went to his vehicle. As he turned the ignition on, immediately a song played on the radio that he had been longing to hear. It was a new song by Kenny G with the chorus 'One more time - yearning for one more hug and kiss.' Rick was overwhelmed with emotion and so grateful to Marlene for that warm and loving message. Later on, after a few months had passed, he had been regularly waking up throughout the night. Restless and stressed, Rick had not had a full nights sleep for some time. Early one morning he woke up suddenly as if something was urging him out of his slumber. As he opened his eyes he glanced to the left side of his bed (the side his late wife used to sleep on). Just at the edge of the bed was an image of a person standing full height. He gazed at the image for a couple of seconds until it faded away. Rick said it appeared to be a female figure but he couldn't be sure if it was his wife because it was still somewhat dark in the room. He reiterated that he knew for certain he was awake and not hallucinating. I informed him that it was common for that to happen, when a spirit tries to appear in the form of an apparition. That it takes an extraordinary amount of energy on their part to come to us in that type of manifestation, and that it was no fault of his that the vision dissipated when it did. That he should be thankful for the visit, which he was. I assured him that Marlene would continue to give him signs of her presence near him and the boys.

Rick also asked me about my opinion on 'eternal marriage.' He had done some reading on this; a philosophy that we are predestined for our partners and that we continue our commitment to each other in a spiritual marriage after we meet our partner on the other side. Rick would like to think that Marlene is in heaven waiting for him and once his jobs and lessons are completed here on earth, that he will join her in heaven where they will continue to be a married couple. My feeling is this...we do pick our lessons we desire to learn and master with each incarnation that we have here on this earthly plane. In chapter 13 I discuss what is called an Akashic Record, or a soul's record of everything that we are and have been, experienced, and learned, as life force energy. I believe we can learn these lessons the hard way or the easy way. Depending on the paths we choose and the choices we make, determine who we meet, how we learn, and where we end up.

Yes chance is possible. There is both good and evil in this world. I do not however consider coincidences as part of the equation. I think there is a higher power at work, shaping, and not so much controlling as instructing how we can improve ourselves and become more in the likeness of God. If we are lucky enough to find someone who we view as our soul mate, and some of us have, I for one am a true believer that that relationship was no accident and that it is primarily why we have such an intense attraction to that individual. Karma teaches us that we come here to remove blockages of past experiences, traumas, phobias, and are given another opportunity to repair, change, and grow from our past experiences. Sometimes a true partner can and does assist you greatly in that process. The love shared between you and your partner or other loved ones is in part because of what you both bring to the table. A balance of each other's idiosyncrasy. A tender patience and at the same time a yearning to discover and experience things together. Each of us learns from the other. I do believe that our higher power, God and our supreme being, knows what and who will be good for us and for getting the most value out of our existence here, and so, introduces and brings together souls in many forms that will do just that. I also am of the opinion that we meet up with our loved ones after we cross to the other side and that our relationships do continue on a soul's level. That we carry on with the dutiful yet loving task of helping one another even over there. I believe we continue to learn and grow spiritually in the afterlife as well. We would have to, to become more in the likeness of God would we not?

Rick felt strongly that God put the two of them together as part of his grand plan. He asked me if I thought that God's plan all along was for Marlene to only be with him until she was forty-eight years of age. Neither he nor Marlene had dated much before being introduced to one another. He had only one girlfriend for a couple of years during high school, and up until then, she had not dated anyone on a steady basis. They had both admitted to having prayed for a mate and found each other at only nineteen years of age. They married when they were twenty-one. Rick said he believed the 'Grand Plan' allowed for them to have six years together to bond as a married couple before they were blessed with their first son. Their marriage was joyful and rich, full of treasured memories.

My response to him was that I find in my line of work, after many sessions and readings with individuals and their families both here and in spirit, that we are all part of some type of plan. That we do, as grueling and challenging as it may be at times, learn and grow through strife and adversity, and that we do reap the benefits of listening to God and spirit, and enjoy the magnificent relationships we are blessed with on our journey to becoming a complete soul. It is not our place to question why, but rather to have faith that there is always a reason!

~ *Psychic Language* ~

Work with the psychic realm is about working with creative process. Thinking outside the box! I read a perfect example of this one day in an email circulating on the net. Here goes…You are driving along in your car on a wild, stormy night. You pass by a bus stop and see three people waiting for the bus. An old lady who looks as if she is about to die, an old friend who once saved your life, and the perfect man (or woman) you have been waiting for all your life. Which one would you choose to offer a ride to, knowing that you could only take one passenger in your car? Think about this for a moment before you continue reading. This is a moral/ethical dilemma that was actually used on part of a job application. You could pick up the old lady afraid of her impending near death and thus you would save her, or you could take the old friend in thanks for once having saved your life. However, you may never be able to find your perfect dream lover again. What do you do? The candidate who was hired (out of 200 applicants) had no trouble coming up with the answer. What did he say? He simply answered; "I would give the car keys to my friend and let him take the old lady to the hospital. I would stay behind and wait for the bus with the woman of my dreams." Now that's thinking outside the box!

Thinking outside the box in a metaphysical sense involves learning to tap into the subconscious mind in a consciously controlled manner. The subconscious mind is the source of your subtle perceptions. It registers everything we encounter, both physical and spiritual. Accessing the subconscious is fundamental for direct spirit communication. Meditation as you have learned earlier is one of the most effective means of awakening your perceptive abilities. When you close your eyes and withdraw your senses from the world around you, you enter another realm of life completely.

In learning to shift the manner in which we perceive the world, we use an altered state of consciousness. We have all experienced altered states. When we dream, read, jog, do repetitious work, take long drives and listen to music, you are in an altered state which 'takes you outside yourself.' These activities produce shifts in consciousness. Through meditation you learn to shift your consciousness in a controlled manner. Visualization is the secret to opening the doors to true spiritual awareness and energies. The spirit realm must take the form of images for us to recognize them and work with them. Meditation is a vital tool for the perceptive abilities of the mind. As you meditate more regularly, you develop and sharpen your language skills with the spirit realm.

Communication with the other side is telepathic. The physical body as we know it has an invisible double, known as the ethereal or astral body. It is an exact duplicate of its physical counterpart. This astral body is our spirit or our soul. In dreams, or what we think of as dreams, the astral body travels about at will, meeting the bodies of others, both living and dead. Memories of these journeys and meetings are what we later recall as dreams. Our astral bodies move with the speed of thought. You must only think you are somewhere and so you are, even if it is half way around the world. Someone once told me to consider the speed of radio waves as an example of how this is possible. Radio waves travel around the world at the speed of light which is 186,000 miles a second. That is the same as traveling four hundred fifty times around the world in one minute! During astral projection, or what we know as an out of body experience, our ethereal double slips out of our physical body and begins to travel but maintains its connection to the physical body with an endless elastic silver-colored cord. During our physical death the spirit separates from the physical body in the same manner only there is no connection, no cord. In instances where a near death experience occurs the cord remains attached.

There is, what I consider, a very funny story concerning an out of body experience, but based on who you ask, you might get another opinion. I was asleep one evening after a very long day that entailed many readings. Depending on the energies I work with that day, I can become very wound up or very drained. This day happened to be the latter. I was utterly exhausted and decided to hit the hay early. I had been asleep for some time when Lou finally crawled in bed next to me. He was just dozing off, eyes closed, when he was overcome by a strange feeling. Not being alarmed in any way but more of a restless sensation, he opened his eyes and turned to look on my side of the bed. Surprised, he found me to be sitting up in bed with my back resting against the headboard. Lou waited for a moment to see if I would say anything to him because he was sure I had seen him turn his head in my direction. As he waited for an explanation of why I was up, he reached out and extended his arm and placed his hand on my shoulder. There was only one slight problem. His hand kept moving and proceeded to pass through my shoulder and then torso until it landed on my face which was actually resting on the pillow! He could now see with focused eyes that my physical body was lying down in bed. It was my astral body that was sitting up! I was startled by his hand falling onto my face and awoke to him yelling, "Wake up Kat, wake up." After he explained why he was in such a state, I began to laugh hysterically. Probably not the most sensitive thing I could have done at the moment, but nonetheless, I found his narrative extremely entertaining. I don't remember that astral experience first hand, but I can tell you that we all have continual occurrences of astral body travel. Some people choose to develop this into a craft where they will travel about at will in a subconscious or trance state and will be able to recount their travels with amazing accuracy. There is a multitude of opportunity when working and exploring the spiritual world. An open mind and intelligent process can lead you in many places and to many experiences.

Spirit, like you in a physical body, can also take many shapes. They will use whatever form is necessary and what that particular spirit is capable of, when deciding which methods to use. Orbs are spirits in the form of balls of light. They are life forms that usually travel in groups and are souls or life force of those that once inhabited a physical body here on earth. Spirit orbs are the most photographed anomalies and are quite photogenic. They can be completely transparent or display themselves in a brightly colored more solid form. It is not hard to capture them on film in their circular form. I have many photos I've taken with my digital camera (no film for you cynics), and caught all types of orbs in shots. They vary in degree in color and size, but most often they appear a more translucent clear ball. Any 35mm camera will work as well. If you go orb hunting, try using at least 800 speed film or higher. The faster the film, the more likely you are to capture an orb. I'm sure that most anyone reading this book has photos in their possession right now which display orbs in the photos. You might just not realize what you were looking at. Some of you have probably thrown pictures away, thinking the white smudges or circles were mistakes that happened when the film was processed by your film developer. Spirits prefer the form of an Orb because it takes less energy, thereby being the form of choice among most. Orbs take up the least amount of energy and apparitions and other fuller shapes take up a great deal more. To paraphrase from the book by Dr. Raymond Moody, *Life After Life*, individuals who have encountered a near death experience have described their spiritual existence as round balls of light and/or energy. As one person recounted regarding their near death experience… "When my heart stopped beating, I felt like I was a round ball and almost maybe like I might have been a little sphere, like a B-B on the inside of this round ball." Another mentioned their recollection as… "I was out of my body looking at it from about ten yards away, but I was still thinking, just like in physical life. And where I was thinking was about my normal body height. I wasn't in a body, as such, I could feel something, like a clear form. I couldn't really see it; it was like it was transparent, but not really. It was like I was just there, an energy maybe, sort of like just a ball of energy. And I really wasn't aware of any bodily sensation, temperature, or anything like that."

Spirits will also show their appearance in the form of ectoplasm mist, as well as full bodied apparitions. Ectoplasm, or sometimes called ecto, has a mist or foggy appearance. It is a smoky grey or white substance which appears to hang or suspend in mid-air and can then dart out in any given direction and dissipate. Your development will usually provide you with the ability to see orbs and ecto in the physical realm. I often see ecto while conducting readings for clients. Although its usual colors are gray or white, ecto has also been seen and photographed in several other colors. These are often picked up on film and video as well, but are rarer.

Vortex, another representation spirit will assume, is an appearance of a swirling funnel shaped vaporous cloud which moves about. Vortexes can appear in pictures as being long and narrow and having a tread like design within their body, as if you captured a small tornado-like object on film. These are also often felt as cold spots. Now that I've described the various images spirit can take let's talk about the language of those on the other side.

- *Symbolism and Communication* -

Everyday we have psychic experiences. It's thinking of someone just as they call on the telephone. Or dreams we have that later reveal themselves as premonitions. It's that gut instinct to go somewhere or do something. Most of us have had a flash of something just before it happens or we say something at exactly the same time as someone else. The most important thing when you're communicating with the other side is to keep an open mind and be willing to accept everything that comes through, even and especially if it doesn't make sense at first.

Be accepting of all the information you are seeing, hearing and feeling when communicating with spirit. Most often when I do readings, a message from spirit will sometimes contain information that the person I'm reading for doesn't recognize. For instance, their brother who is passed throws out a specific date of August 16th. They swear to you that they do not know what he's referring to. Yet, when they later check with other family members or friends, they are told that August 16th was an anniversary of an event which took place while the brother was still alive. The person I was reading for was just unaware of this particular date. So no matter what information you get from the other side, please pass it on. If the person you are reading for doesn't recognize it, tell them to check out the details with family members or friends. They'll find it will always be validated in some way. When I first started giving readings it was sometimes difficult to not only understand what the spirit was saying but also how to deliver the information. Whenever I caught myself censoring the message, it would always be revealed later in the reading. For instance, I was doing a reading for a man named Fred. He was there to connect with his sister. She came through right away and the reading was going fairly well with good validations that Fred was feverishly writing down. I was then shown a badge and I asked the spirit what type of badge it was? I couldn't quite make it out, but knew that it was a badge of some kind. Fred's sister didn't offer anything other than showing me a horse. So I skipped over the badge and only spoke of the horse that she was showing me. When I asked Fred if he recognized a horse connection to his sister, he replied "Yes," and the reading continued. His sister got across that he had a birthday coming up, that their mother had moved to a new home, and that Fred had recently taken a new position at his bank. After all of those messages though, she referred back to the badge showing it to me again only this time making it bigger and bigger. I finally asked Fred, "Why does your sister keep showing me this thing that looks like a badge? I cannot make out what type it is, if it's law enforcement, fire department or what. She's made it fuzzy so I can't quite make it out. Do you know what she means?" "Why, yes," he retorted loudly. "She's talking about her horse! Her horse's name was Badge!" I felt terrible. Here she had given me the information earlier when showing me the horse in the beginning of the reading, but because I was selfish and wanted her to answer for me what type of badge it was, I didn't pass the information along to Fred. At the time I wanted more…sometimes that's all there is. It's important to pass on *exactly* what it is they're showing or telling you!

Spirits use the language of symbolism to communicate. You may hear words or see images. You may feel sensations, or many times spirits impress upon you physical pain to show how they crossed over. This is not the same type of physical pain you are used to experiencing though. This pain felt through clairsentience is something that you totally control and can shut off at any time. I was once at a psychic fair where I did a reading for two sisters. Sitting in front of me, they were optimistic of who might come through and were very eager to get started. As we began, a young man came through in his early twenties that described in detail the trip they had just returned from in Arkansas. He told them of the mountainous place where they had stayed and that their mother had accompanied them on the trip as well. He identified himself as an old college classmate of one of the sisters. She explained that he had died tragically while they were still in school. She was very surprised to see him come through after so many years, but glad that he had made the appearance. As he was pulling his energy back and I waited patiently for the next spirit to come through, I placed my hands flat on the table. All of a sudden simultaneously, I saw the vision of an older woman, very stern looking, and a sharp pain which started at my shoulder shot down my left arm and out through my ring finger with such force that my hand literally jumped off the table. The sisters jumped, I yelled a very loud "ouch" and began shaking my left hand as if to shake off the pain. "What was that?" One of the sisters asked. "You have an older female coming through who claims to have lost part of her ring finger! And boy of all the ways she could have communicated this to me, she sure picked a mean way to do it!" Well, I no sooner got the words out of my mouth when they both in unison covered their mouths and gasped! "Oh no…" one of the sisters said, "We don't want to hear from her!" With that response I couldn't help but laugh and asked why. "That's our grandmother. She was always very mean to us. We don't want to speak to her. We want to hear from our other grandmother!" Fortunately that is all that grandmother had to say and she left as quickly as she came. Interesting, that sometimes spirits are very good at retaining their old personalities. This shows you that sometimes even over there, spirits are still learning life lessons they failed to learn here.

Back to sensing, you may smell fragrances or odors, which also remind you of the person on the other side. Sometimes the messages come through clearly and accurately, leaving no room for interpretation. But most of the time, we must unravel exactly what it is they're trying to say. Some of the symbols I have gotten remain consistent, like usually when I hear a number, it means they're referring to a significant event that took place or is about to take place, like a birthday, anniversary, death date, or wedding date, on that date, or during the month of that number. For example, if they say or show me a four, it either means they're referring to the fourth month April, or the fourth of a month. Remember to write down whatever you get and check it out later. I'll tell you the symbols I see, hear, and feel most often, but stay open to the possibility that you might receive new symbols specific to you.

Above means that the spirit is older than the sitter being read in some way: parents, grandparents, older friends or relatives. To the side refers to a spirit or person who is the same age as the sitter who is being read such as a sibling, friend, cousin, etc. Below is younger than the sitter being read: a child or younger sibling or friend. A white rose is a sign of congratulations, usually signifying a birthday, new baby or a marriage. A red rose is spirit expressing their love to the sitter. If there are thorns on it, there was tension between the sitter or someone the sitter knows and the spirit. The spirit, when here on earth, was probably unable to express their love properly. A parallel line between the spirit and the sitter means they share something similar such as same name, interests or may look alike in physical appearance. When I see black spots that usually indicates cancer. Flowing blood means the cause of death was some type of blood disorder like diabetes, leukemia, AIDS, etc. Again, numbers mean important dates like birth, death or other significant dates. Sometimes spirits will give you zodiac signs to signify a month. Spirit will at times give a clearly recognizable name, an initial of the first name, or especially if it is a strange sounding or uncommon name, a 'sounds like' to convey the name. They will also use a middle name of the person they are calling to or trying to say when there is another family member with the same name. Names can be heard, but sometimes you may just get the sound of the name or the first couple letters. For example, if you hear Ray, it could be Fay, but most often what I hear is the sound of a name. Stock images would be badges such as law enforcement or security, uniforms like fire, police, military, doctor, nurse, sports, or circus, etc. Bells usually signify a wedding or a celebration of some kind. A key might indicate success with a situation.

Pay attention to specks of light. Seeing specks of light shows progress in spiritual and psychic development. When you start developing your psychic gifts, spirit tends to reward you with this. A bright light or even speck of light is most often a spirit trying to communicate with you or get your attention. While meditating one evening in my office, I became thirsty and went downstairs for a drink. When returning to my office, which is on the second floor, I started up the stairs and noticed three very small balls of light in front of my stomach area. They were approximately eight to ten inches in front of me, and began moving slowly as if dancing around each other. I stood there on the staircase frozen and watched as they bounced and moved in rhythm. Blinking hard to make sure it wasn't my eyes playing tricks on me, the three lights stayed right where they were but moved over and over each other. I decided to slowly make my way up to the second floor and see if they moved with me. Much to my astonishment, they did, only as we began our journey up they started turning into color. One light pink, one pale blue, and one a pale yellow. Now I am really freaking out. I was so excited I was sure that I would kill this illustrious moment because of the amount of energy I was giving off. Quite the contrary. They continued to dance over one another and playfully led me down the hallway to my office. As I crossed the threshold of my office door they dissolved. I promptly thanked my spirit guides for giving me that wonderful and inspiring experience.

Synonymous items are a common way for spirit to get their idea across. For instance, they will often-time show you movie actors, movie titles, landmarks in your town or around the country such as Mount Rushmore, songs, particular flowers, or anything to get you to say what they want to convey. Sometimes being shown a daisy, rose, or lily might not be a flower at all, but rather someone's name; Daisy, Rose or Lily. Communication with the other side is tricky for sure, but with practice, you and your guides will not only develop a rapport, but a method of language that is unique to you and them. Your guides are fully aware of what you will respond to. It's up to you to be consistent with your interpretations and still remain open to variances.

In understanding the metaphysical world, we should ascertain that synergy is a key player in the agenda that for every action in the universe there is an equal and opposite reaction. Take an event which happened in Six Mile, Alabama in November of 2002. Six Mile is approximately 60 miles south of Birmingham. Two sisters, Sheila Wentworth, 45 years old and Doris Hall, 52 years old, each left their respective homes to surprise the other with a visit at exactly 4:00PM. They both owned the same type of vehicle, a Jeep Cherokee. Highway 25, in rural Alabama, connects them. On their way to each other's home and steaming toward each other from opposite ends of the county, the Jeep Cherokees carrying the two women approached a bend in the road. They collided head-on. Varying official reports clocked their speed at anywhere from 60 to 100 mph. Consider the odds of this event taking place. What adds to the mysticism of this tragedy is what put the two sisters on the road that day, routine. They were doing what they always did. Their eleven brothers and sisters inhabit the hills around them. This is very familiar territory. Neither sister worked anymore. Both had married young, and chose big men who labored in factories. Happily, they would often drive miles to visit each other and share a cup of coffee and reminisce. Highway 25 linked them together. It is a beautiful stretch of pavement that runs for about 50 miles, one lane each way. What's even more peculiar is this highway was a familiar place of misfortune for these sisters. In 1973, Talmadge Smith, the sister's father, died of a heart attack along Highway 25. Then in 1982, Doris Hall was driving with her son, Bo, when they skidded off a bridge and into a creek. Bo, only 12 years of age then, bent the door open and sat his mother on top of the car to keep her from drowning. That accident happened just a mere 100 yards from where their two Jeeps slammed into each other. The day was overcast, but dry. There seems to be no apparent reason why these two vehicles collided. All they know for sure is that one of the vehicles crossed the center line, colliding with the other. Billy Joe Hall Jr., Doris' husband also died in the accident.

There are other forces at play sometimes, and no matter what we do, there will come a time when we all must meet our Maker. I am of the belief that we choose our time of physical death before coming here, and I have witnessed many times where tell tale signs are given by those who go on before us, showing that on a soul's level, individuals know they are about to cross over. They give off certain behavior to indicate this. I was made painfully aware of that with my friend, Paul's passing.

I am a regularly invited guest on a local radio show in Dallas. Once a month I connect people with their loved ones in spirit across the air waves. While discussing synergy on the show, one of the listeners called in to share her story of a synchronous event that in her words, "Really freaked her out." Seems she was driving home along highway 635 which is a major thoroughfare in Dallas. She happened upon the scene of what was obviously, a recent accident. She saw no medical vehicles, and by the looks of the cars involved, she knew it was a serious situation. Pulling her car to the side of the road, she jumped out to see if there was anything she could do. Running up to one of the vehicles, she found a woman in grave distress. The good samaritan did her best to administer CPR but the woman unfortunately died. An entire year later, she was sitting in her home with her significant other, when he announced that a friend, whom he hadn't seen in some time, was coming over to visit. When his friend arrived, they all began playing the "get-to-know-you-game," sharing stories of their upbringing and family history, etc. As the friend told of his mother's passing, she was shocked to find him describing the very accident she had stopped at the year before. As it turned out it was this friend's mother who she had tried to save! Again, what are the odds?

There is an obvious motive and more to these relationships than what is understood at first glance. Now apply this line of thinking as sheer faith in understanding and believing the sometimes wacky messages we receive from spirit. When you are channeling, meditating, or however you are communicating with spirit, remember that they understand at a higher, and more complicated level the domino effect of our actions and thoughts here on earth. That life is exponential and that what we do today helps to shape what happens tomorrow. Therefore, if we just listen and learn from what they are telling us, we will go a lot farther in interpreting their meanings and in turn they will be able to better guide us in the directions necessary for our individual growth.

A good example of this happened to me one evening while painting a crib for my daughter. She was expecting triplets and we all pitched in whatever way possible. As I sat there on my kitchen floor, covered in paint, newspapers strewn about and diligently painting, I began revisiting the events of that day. Quietly thinking to myself conversations I had had, you know, just rehashing what I had accomplished. What was unordinary is that I caught myself thinking in an English accent! I stopped painting, chuckled and laughed it off and went back to work with the brush strokes. Sure enough, about ten minutes later, there I am again repeating conversations from earlier in my head, yet in this English accent. Now you would've thought I would be keener than that by now, but hey, we're all human. I finally woke up and realized that spirit was trying to get my attention. "Boy…" I thought, "What could this be about?" Sitting there on the kitchen floor, I invited spirit in to see if there was a message here and what it was they were trying to tell me. All I kept receiving was this 'desperate' feeling. As if I was on the cusp of something really strong and traumatic yet no specific, detailed information was actually given to me. After trying for several minutes, I decided that if they needed to get an explicit message across they would find a way, and went back to finishing the crib. The next morning when checking my email I received my answer.

"Dear Kathleen,
Hi, my name is Sandy. I'm having an extremely tough time dealing with my mum's death. I've tried so hard to communicate with her and I can't go on. I quit working two years ago to help my dad take care of her and had a special bond with her. I don't know if she knew I was there. A lot of times I want to end everything and go to the other side to be with her. My mum was my life. My family was all at her bedside when she passed and my sister said all of a sudden she felt a calming feeling come over her. Why didn't I? I totally lost it and wouldn't let go of my mum. Is there any possible way you could give me a reading? I would be so extremely grateful and maybe I could learn to get on with my life and live instead of just existing and crying every day. I know I am asking a lot of you and I'm sorry but I don't

know what else to do. I fully understand if you can't help me talk
to my mum and that is okay. Thanks for at least just listening.
Eagerly awaiting your response.
Love,
Sandy"

Needless to say I didn't even bother to check the rest of
my emails and immediately responded to hers, telling her how
her mother had visited me the night before. We spoke later that
day, and during Sandy's reading her mother came through loud
and clear. It seemed to offer Sandy a great deal of comfort
knowing that her mother had gone to great lengths to link her
and me together. That her mother was indeed aware of her
feeling of hopelessness and had reached out to her offering her
support even from the beyond. I am forever amazed at the power
of spirit and their ability to move mountains, conjure events, and
manipulate situations to accomplish their goals. Sometimes I feel
we are but pawns in a vast sea of spiritual antiquity. And I'm
okay with that.

~ *Meeting Your Guides and Vibrating To Spirit* ~

For those of you who have skipped right to this chapter...be aware that cheating never works! I say that tongue in cheek, but I am honest when I tell you that you will not succeed in this process if you have not read the previous chapters. I repeat over and over in my psychic development classes, that one of the keys to increasing your awareness is the desire to do so, but with this comes responsibility. High integrity on the part of the psychic is paramount for achievement. Each story I've written has a lesson attached to it.

Before I get into exactly how you go about meeting your guides, I want to help you understand a little more about the fundamentals of the metaphysical. I believe reincarnation is real. I also believe that the rate at which souls incarnate determines their rate of growth and evolution. There is no right or wrong, better or worse in the process of reincarnating, but at what speed we incarnate will be determined by the acceptance of knowledge and understanding concerning our soul's journey. In other words, what we learn along the way in each incarnation determines to what level our soul elevates each time we cross over.

I think the purpose of reincarnation is for you to discover, study, and experience who you are through lifetime after lifetime, striving to be in the likeness of God. Your purpose as a soul is to come to the realization that you are part of God. That we are all pieces of a large puzzle God has created as a vehicle by which we can continue to explore and learn from every situation and from each person we meet. We are evolving as souls and consciousness constantly. What we are evolving towards is not the focus. It is the journey that is the focus.

The purpose of experiencing a lifetime after lifetime is so the soul will realize who it is and where it came from. To learn life lessons of unconditional love, and praise. When we examine the concept of reincarnation, it is equally important to look at the laws of karma. Karma is the universal law of cause and effect. This cause and effect seems to be, what *is* the universe. There is a lot of misconception about karma and exactly what it does. Karma has long been associated with raising fear. Folklore teaches that karma is a retribution system of weights and measures. Not really true. I believe each one of us has free will and the freedom to choose how to grow. We may decide to grow with joy, or alternatively, through pain, distress and fear. The law of karma is not a justice system, but rather a check and balance structure that we can tap into in overcoming past mistakes and repairing obstructions that create bad decision making. For instance a person who has endured a lot of suffering in this lifetime is not a victim of 'bad karma', but simply finds themselves in predicaments that are the result of their own beliefs about themselves. By being trapped in bad decision making, and refusal to accept and grow through your experiences, souls can carry around imbalance and strife with them for many lifetimes. Another example is if an individual should deeply hurt another, it is not the deed itself that attracts the karma; it is the emotional state and the beliefs about the self that led to the act of wrong doing in the first place. This belief system will create the karma or result, at a future date, whether that date is in the present or a future life. Anything we have ever experienced, in this lifetime or past lifetimes, is contained in our soul's Akashic record.

Phobias, repeated life patterns, unexplained fears such as vertigo, and déjà vu are all part of obstacles we create from past-life experiences. These obstacles can manifest subtly or very dramatically in our lives, depending on the depth of the belief that caused the hindrance. However on the flip side, we have the opportunity to clear these obstacles and free ourselves from the effects of past-life karma. Karma does equal punishment. In contrast, the law of karma is a law of love, and it searches to release us from our past.

Consider everything about you, who you are, and what you do is energy. Energy can neither be created nor destroyed, it only changes form. So every loving thought as well as every fearful thought causes an effect. Effects stay connected to their causes. When we choose these thoughts they stay connected to our ego-self. Therefore, painful experiences can stay joined to us. One after another, in a seemingly endless cycle for as long as we stay connected to the cause or the fearful thoughts. But, if we release the cause, the effect is released as well. Releasing karma simply requires releasing false ideas, which are causing painful effects. Changing your perspective, goals and desires will bring about change and opportunity. Mistakes do not require punishment, they simply require correction. As you do this your soul will begin an evaluation which encompasses all of your lives, experiences and quests on all planes of existence. Your soul commits to a sequence of incarnations until it has accomplished bringing its higher levels of consciousness into one. Again, creating itself in the exact likeness of God.

Let's talk about our soul's record. The Akashic Record is the individual record of a soul experienced with each incarnation in a physical life. It is believed that at the time we make the decision to experience life on the earthly plane there is a field of energy created to record every thought, word, emotion and action generated by that experience. This field of energy is called the Akashic Record. Akashic, because it is composed of Akasha, the energetic substance believed to be from which all life is formed and Record, because its objective is to record all life experience.

Every movement, thought, or action is transmitted to subconscious levels. These events witnessed, observed, or even imagined are recorded upon this substance known as Akasha. Some people call it the light of God. I interpret it as a tool by which God records what the soul does. If your interest in the metaphysical involves astrology, charts and the like, you might be destined to do more research into Akasha. There is much that can be learned from studying the various writings and viewpoints on what Akasha is. Information about Akashic Records or sometimes referred to also as the Book of Life, can be found in folklore, myth, and throughout the Old and New Testaments in the Bible. It is traceable at least as far back as the Semitic peoples and includes the Arabs, the Assyrians, the Phoenicians, the Babylonians, and the Hebrews. Each of these groups believed that there was in existence a sort of celestial documentation which contained the history of both humankind and information on spiritual existence.

There is a reference in scripture found in Exodus 32:32. After the Israelites had committed a most grievous sin by worshiping the golden calf, it was Moses who pleaded on their behalf, offering to take full responsibility and have his own name stricken out of thy book which thou hast written in compensation for their deed. Later, in the Old Testament, the Bible says there is nothing about an individual that is not known in this same book. In Psalm 139, David makes reference to the fact that God has written down everything about him and all the details of his life, even that which is imperfect and those deeds which have yet to be performed. I believe that everything written is interpretive and you should make your own judgments based on your individual belief system. I am simply sharing mine with you and what I have found recognizable in translation with what I believe God and my spirit guides have shown me.

With regard to more contemporary phenomena, possibly the most profound source of information regarding the Akashic Record comes from the work of Edgar Cayce. Edgar Cayce lived from 1877 to 1945 and was a devout Christian and Psychic. History shows that for most of his adult life, he possessed the mysterious ability to put himself into a kind of an altered state in which virtually any type of information was available to him about the person he was reading for. There are a plethora of biographies and hundreds of other books written about his case studies and the extreme accuracy of Cayce's psychic work. These books explore the various aspects of his information and the thousands of topics he discussed. He would often time diagnose and sometimes even provide a cure for his patients when he and they were hundreds of miles apart. When asked where the source of information came from for these remarkable readings, Cayce replied that there were basically two. The first was the subconscious mind of the individual for whom he was giving the reading, and the second was the individual's Akashic Record.

Is not God's main message love all things, for in all things is Love? Our Akashic Record when used as a teacher and guide allows us to know our karmic imbalances and helps us remember our experiences. In all moments we have the choice to think, feel and act in a loving way or not. It is always our choice. When working with your psychic senses, make it a priority to purify all frequencies through visualization in order to return to a full awareness of God. I believe that this is our purpose for learning life lessons on earth. Use the Akasha Record as the teacher which helps you remember all things. Remember, learn and grow from your past actions.

- *Spirit Guides and Guardian Angels* -

Have you ever had a dream that seemed especially vivid and real in which you met a wise man, woman or animal with whom you felt an immediate sense of warm acceptance and connection? You might have been meeting an angel or spirit guide! My guides first appeared to me in dreams. They will sometimes first appear to you during meditation. I have found that they determine when and how they appear to us. Based on many factors such as your openness to their presence, your ability to recognize them, or maybe their preference of where it might be easier to communicate with you. I also feel their presence around me in everyday living. Sometimes they make themselves known visually where I see sparks of light. This usually happens when they are trying hard to get my attention or in times when I need to know they are supporting me or my thought process. Guides can also make themselves known through synchronicity, the meaningful coincidences that lead you to people, places or events that turn out to have special significance in your life. Most times all that is needed to make contact with your guides is the sincere desire to do so. It's that simple. Prayer and ritual are essential ways to invite spirit helpers into your life. Learning to interpret the symbols in dreams and synchronous events or learning to meditate, visualize, and channel information is necessary to communicate with your spirit guides.

We may often experience spirit contact in our lives but fail to recognize it for what it is. This chapter will help you learn to access and tune into your guardian angels and spirit guides, as well as family and friends after their physical death. Through a series of simple exercises, you can safely and gradually increase your awareness of spirit and your ability to identify them. You will learn to develop an intentional and directed communication skill with the other side.

A spirit guide is an evolved being and in some cases was once perhaps in a physical form. Although angelic in nature, spirit guides are free will entities and have chosen their path of further growth. A spirit guide may even be a close relative or friend who has passed. If they were very spiritual on earth, there is a strong possibility they are still assisting you from the other side. If you suspect that one of your guides is a past relative, during meditation ask that spirit guide to identify themselves using a symbol of your choice or one they give to you. If this is the case, they will use that identifier over and over to let you know it is them around you. For instance, if you think uncle Harry may be a suspected guide, tell him to make your fingers tingle, or maybe feel a hand on your shoulder. Rely on your intuition. If you feel something is a sign from them, write down how, where and when it happens. See if this sign is consistent whenever you feel or call their presence around you. If it truly is them, they will be consistent in what they do to communicate that to you. With practice you will learn to sense when they are present.

You have many spirit guides. Some are master teachers and some not. All guides are here to direct and teach you when you are willing to listen. They are always communicating to you through your thoughts, music, your environment, wherever they need to be in order to communicate a message to you. Each individual spirit guide you have serves a specific need for your growth. When you have accomplished a specific goal, or learned a specific lesson, you may no longer need that particular guide and they will move on to assist someone new. As you learn life's lessons and your needs change, so do your guides.

Everyone has a guardian angel. I believe some of us have multiple guardian angels. Your guardian angel is dedicated to you throughout your lifetime here. They travel with you on every journey that you, as a free will entity, make. From what I have gathered and learned through readings and from spirits on the other side, your guardian angel makes an agreement with your soul to assist it in completing any task it has decided to undertake. This means that before coming to earth, and when choosing the lessons you wanted to learn in this lifetime, your guardian angel was along side you. They agreed to serve and protect you throughout your entire lifetime here. I consider this the reason we hear of miraculous rescues and heroic saves of people here on the earthly plane who find themselves in situations of great peril. If a soul has decided to remain focused on the earth plane for a specific length of time, a guardian angel will assist in getting someone out of trouble whose time is not up. Your guardian angel is your supreme protector and custodian. Your spirit guide on the other hand, is here to assist you in making easier choices that will help you to grow through experiences with less difficulty. That is why when we refuse to listen to the signs and symbols we're shown by our guides, we often must learn things the hard way.

Communicating with spirit is a skill that can be achieved by anyone with the sheer desire and determination to do so. Those who have crossed over are on the astral plane. By connecting with your spirit guides, they will deliver to you in the form of signs and symbols, the messages from those on the other side. When I am conducting a reading whether it is a group or individual session, I am incorporating the assistance of God, my spirit guides, the spirit guides of the person I am reading for, and the spirit of loved ones crossed over. All of these elements are working together to provide the clearest channel of communication possible.

Communicating with spirit you'll find also helps you to exist more in tune with your higher self, because your guides are contacted through that part of you which is your higher consciousness. This interprets to thinking in an elevated and clearer manner as your relationships with your spirit guides develop.

Spirit guides are here to help you lift the veil between your world and theirs. It's important to them that your intention to grow spiritually is sincere. Suffice to say, if you are developing your psychic skills for the sole purpose of making money, you will fail. There is a great responsibility that goes hand in hand when performing psychic work. Increase your skills out of a desire to elevate yourself spiritually and you will go far. Do it to achieve the lessons you signed up for when in soul form and you will raise your soul to a new plane when you cross over.

When doing this type of spiritual work, communicating with the dead, many of you may have fears of attracting negative entities. Poltergeists, ghosts stuck on this plane, or specters as they are sometimes called, do exist. But you are always in total control of the process. When you meditate and channel spirit, you simply always ask, think, deliberately, and intuitively know you are only contacting divine spirit and spirit that is good, not evil! Just as I said before, no being of energy can contact you without your asking or requesting it to do so. Therefore, when you ask to speak to spirit, your intuitive thoughts and intentions and vibrations are felt and known in the universe. Only Godly spirit and those spirits that are good intentioned will be drawn to you. And don't concern yourself worrying about whether any of your guides will play tricks on you or mislead you. Your spirit guide will not lie about itself, or deceive you in any way. Their only intention is to make your journey here closer to God and reach those on a pure spiritual realm, as easy and successful as possible.

Start the process of communicating with your guide while you are in deep meditation. Relax using your rhythmic breathing, then focus on increasing your vibration level and simply state clearly that you wish to speak to your spirit guides. Try to intuitively visualize a guide or a being of light standing in front of you. It's okay if you see only darkness when first attempting to meet your guides. Everyone is different and will therefore experience different things. Meeting your guides takes a lot of practice. You may or may not actually see something right away. You will however, feel or intuitively know what your guide looks like, and if and when they are present. Once you sense your guide is there, ask for your guide's name. Perhaps ask some of the questions I gave you in chapter 10, and then wait patiently for an answer. It may even sound like you are answering yourself. The key is to trust the first answer you hear! This is always the right answer.

Once you have made mental contact with a guide in meditation, you are now ready to attempt to communicate with other spirits. Keep practicing and don't give up. Your guides will give you the assistance necessary for you to hear spirit and those that have crossed over when they know you are truly ready. By that, I mean ready to accept the responsibility of understanding the messages, and being a good interpreter of the information.

Ask your guides, angels, and God to assist you in hearing from those individuals you desire. Be open to receiving any visions, thoughts, smells, and feelings from those on the other side. When first starting, you might have someone else there to write down anything that comes through. Or if you're alone, keep a tape recorder or pad and pen available to record what you experience. It will be important to reflect on what happens in each session as you grow spiritually. As time passes you will not only be able to see a progression in your ability, but also start to connect signs and symbols from your loved ones and spirit guides. With practice you will learn to recognize these symbols and be able to interpret them faster. You will also be able to spend more time focusing on deciphering what it is you are getting from them. If you are bringing through spirit for another person, never try to distinguish which messages you give to that person. Always give them every message, sign, feeling, and symbol that comes through. You have seen from some of the stories I've shared with you, that oftentimes the simplest message can have an enormous meaning. You will be amazed at what a small, seemingly insignificant symbol may mean to you, yet it means so much to the individual you're reading for. Also when doing readings for others, you'll find times when they are unable to validate the information you are receiving from someone in spirit. Tell them to just write it down and then check with other family members or friends. They will find someone to validate it, I promise. The spirit knows what it is trying to say. The person you're doing the reading for, just might not be aware of what the message means. That is, until it is delivered to the proper person for whom it was intended! Never doubt spirit and always trust what you are receiving. Learn to master those two things and you will become a successful reader and medium.

- Developing a Trigger -

Once you have found that you can successfully communicate with both your spirit guides and loved ones on other side, you can work on developing what's called a trigger. Most psychic mediums work this into their process of reaching the spiritual realm. Many of you will probably do it unconsciously. But learning to use a trigger in a controlled way provides you with a fast lane, if you will, to the spirit world. Triggers are very easy to develop. Remember that anything we do on a consistent basis becomes habit. Something we do routinely will become buried in our subconscious. Walking up a flight of stairs and not having to physically gaze at each individual stair as you go up, is one example. Your feet intuitively know what to do because this is buried in your subconscious from years of walking up stairs.

To develop a trigger, perform the following exercise. This can be used anytime you would like to go into an instant condition of readiness to speak with spirit while in a conscious state. Let's say that I wanted to use the trigger that every time I rubbed my hands together, I would automatically go into a state of conscious trance, a condition of relaxation that would open my subconscious mind to receive information. Now that I know what will trigger this state in me, I have to reinforce this on a consistent basis so that it will become routine.

Sit quietly and take a few deep breaths. Allow your body and mind to become one. As you are relaxing, say silently to yourself, "Every time I rub my hands together, I will go into an open receptive state." Say this several times as you rub your hands together. You should be focusing, as you are relaxing, on increasing your vibration level. Begin using your visualization exercise used to increase your vibrations you learned in Chapter 10. Remember, you must increase your vibrational speed, and spirit must decrease theirs, in order to meet to communicate. You should start to feel your adrenaline pumping and have an excited feeling. Stay with that feeling and continue your visualization, increasing your vibrations faster and faster. Now start sensing, using the five psychic senses, and your guides will be around you ready to assist you in talking to spirit. When you are finished, bring yourself back into a fully conscious state by saying silently to yourself, "At the count of three, I will become fully awake and alert." Touch something solid around you to ground yourself, and always thank spirit for their assistance. It's that easy.

A trigger becomes part of us on a subconscious level. It uses a physical conditioning that is then developed into a subconscious habit. When a trigger is initiated, it will open the pathway to speak to spirit because that is what you have trained it to do. A trigger is one more way to communicate with those in the spirit realm in a managed and controlled setting. Using the trigger technique you will now be able to turn your psychic gift of hearing spirit on and off at will.

~ *Tools For Intuition* ~

There are many forms of divination. Divination is the use of a ritual to discover hidden knowledge by spiritual means. I will explain the purpose and practice of a few forms of divination in this chapter to assist you in developing your relationship with spirit. These rituals are designed to help you learn to recognize spirit (whether it's your guides or loved ones) and understand the means of communication spirit may use. When you attend church you enjoy worshiping with others, find comfort in being in the spiritual house of your God, and sense the reassurance felt from maintaining roots and history in that church over a period of time. When you are in church there are many elements happening in which you are probably unaware. For instance, did you know that when you repeatedly say the same liturgies week after week, you are elevating yourself to a higher consciousness? Bringing your consciousness and subconscious closer together allows you to operate in a higher state of vibration. You will have increased awareness of the two worlds, both physical and spiritual, working together. This is why the act of ritual is important. Anything we do on a continual basis becomes buried in our subconscious. Your subconscious is from where you speak to spirit.

- *The Tarot* -

The tarot is an instrument that allows us direct access to knowledge stored in our subconscious. It is the language of our intuition and premonitions. When we consult the tarot, it tells us about our feelings and worries and gives us information and answers. In other words, tarot cards are a way of gaining insight into our spiritual and earthly worlds. Our spirit guides can use this as a means of communicating to us an understanding of what is happening in our lives. For each question, there is an immediate answer. When doing readings for yourself or others, please limit it to one reading per day. More than one per day will run the risk of inaccuracy and confusion.

- Card Interpretations -

The tarot card deck contains 78 cards that are divided into two main groups. The 22 Major Arcana cards and the 56 Minor Arcana cards. The Major Arcana pertains to strong outside influences, while the Minor Arcana reveals what is taking place in your day to day life.

The Major Arcana disclose the larger areas of your life in a reading. They also teach you lessons and guidance regarding your weaknesses and strengths.

The Minor Arcana is divided into four groups; Cups, Pentacles, Swords, and Wands. Here is a brief explanation of each group along with a keyword which is the origin of that group. Cups that appear in a reading indicate the type of emotion around the question. They may also indicate family matters and how one reacts to those family matters. Cups keyword is spirituality. Pentacles represent our financial situation in a reading. They also indicate how we react to our finances as well as whether money plays a significant part of our past, present or future. Keywords for pentacles are money and material things. Swords in a reading show us action or inaction in regards to a question. They may also indicate with what degree of force the movement with someone entering or leaving our lives will be. Keywords for swords are drive and ambition. Wands show us strength or weakness in regards to our question. They will show character as well. The keyword for wands is creativity.

- *Storing Your Cards* -

You want to impress your energy on your cards. When you first receive your deck, sleep with them under your pillow and carry them with you in your purse or briefcase. You want to build a close relationship with these cards. When they are not in use, I recommend you place them in a dark cloth bag, preferably violet or indigo color (one of the top chakra colors), and place them in a wooden box (the wood acts as a grounding device).

- *Reading the Cards* -

When doing a reading for yourself, make sure that you review your situation thoroughly. Think about all of the people that may be involved, directly or indirectly. You want to examine your problem without judgment. Clear your mind and focus. Focus on the directions for that particular reading. Choose a card spread which is a particular pattern in which you lay the cards, that you feel best fits your question. Most of these card patterns will be found in your booklet that came with your deck and in any tarot handbook you buy. Rely on your guides and intuition. Your subconscious will steer you. The tarot interpretation, like any other technique, becomes more interesting with practice. As you memorize the meanings of the cards, your intuition and psychic abilities take over and your interpretation will hold increased accuracy. One easy way to learn the tarot without having to memorize all seventy-eight cards at once is to do daily five card spreads. It is very difficult for most of us to learn seventy-eight meanings right away and this causes most people to give up before they ever really learn the tarot. With only looking up five meanings a day, and learning the tarot over a period of time, you allow yourself to really absorb the meanings and build a good relationship and intuitive understanding of your deck. As with learning any new language, determination is essential and the tarot symbols are nothing more than the language vehicle that spirit uses to guide us.

- Cards That Jump Out While Shuffling -

As you are shuffling, one or two cards may seem to jump out of the deck. Your guides are pushing these cards at you for a reason, so set those cards aside. These cards have significance pertaining to the reading. Study them before proceeding with your card spread. You will find those cards will have dominant features which help to decipher and bring about a clearer interpretation.

When reading for someone else, ask your sitter (the person requesting the reading) to shuffle the cards until they feel satisfied, then cut them into 3 stacks. In this way, the cards are impressed by energy from the sitter. You then restack the cards in whichever order calls to you. Next, deal the cards into the spread. Then interpret the cards using your psychic insights, knowledge of the cards, and the position of cards. After a card spread reading, ask your sitter for specific questions they need answers to that may not have been covered in the original spread. Pull three cards only for each question asked, and read again to get your answers.

In the tarot, it is sometimes difficult to give time frames. Experience has shown me that time frames in the tarot can be immediate and can also predict events as far in the future as years ahead. What are important are the intuitive impressions you receive when asking for a specific time frame. Rely on your first inclination. It is always the correct answer.

When you read for others, ask them to try not to share any family history, money matters, health issues, or other personal information which may influence your ability to give them an accurate reading. If you're reading for a close friend or relative, just try to maintain objectivity and under no circumstances, should you hold back any information from them. Regardless of your feelings for the sitter, it is your responsibility to relay any information you're given by either the cards or directly from your guides, to them. It is not your role to play God. There is a great responsibility that goes with tarot or any other tools used to pass on messages from the other side. Have high standards and moral ethics in everything that you do involving your psychic work.

- Automatic Writing -

When we talk about automatic writing, we are talking about channeling. We are allowing information to come from spirit and through our hand from the other side. This is a wonderful tool that can be done on a paper source or at your computer keyboard. It involves consciously shifting your mind into your psychic place while still staying in a conscious state. To allow your guides, loved ones or others in spirit in, you can use either your progressive relaxation exercise or your trigger technique. It's up to you. You need to get your own thoughts out of the way and become receptive to their higher vibration.

When you begin a session, make sure it is at a time when you will not be disturbed or interrupted for at least fifteen to twenty minutes. Using your protection exercise, welcome vibrational spirit into your session by performing your affirmation and prayer. End the session in the same way. Some of you will experience your hand taking off immediately. Others will be making circles and it will seem like nothing is coming through. Be patient. If you're just getting circles but receiving strong mental messages, then go ahead and write them down. Sometimes when you write it down it will lead you into full automatic writing. Most individuals will experience loops, circles and what appears to be scribbling at first. As time progresses and you continue practicing, you will get small words and phrases, then eventually sentences. If a computer is your writing instrument of choice, you will have the same results. You'll start slowly and eventually experience rapid fire communication through clairsentience and your other four psychic senses.

Some people have found that they are more successful in automatic writing when they occupy their conscious side in another activity such as watching television, reading a book, etc. This helps to distract from the subconscious and keeps an open channel for spirit to communicate. Personally I have tried it both ways and find that concentrating on my meditation and visualization exercise while doing automatic writing is more rewarding and produces better results. There is no right or wrong way to do auto writing, just experiment and find what works for you.

- Steps to a Session -

1. Write the date at the top of your paper.
2. Have a clear question of what you want information on.
3. Be clear about whom you wish to come through. If your desire is to just simply hear from your guides, state so.
4. Either go through a body relaxation, or use a trigger to put yourself into your psychic place.
5. Bring in the white light of protection.
6. Ask your guides, masters, or whoever you wish to communicate with, to join you. Have them sign in and then sign

out when the session is through. This will give you an indication of who you are communicating with.

7. While holding your pen (felt tip glides easier) or pencil with a very limp wrist, making sure to keep your arm off of the table, wait for their response. If you prefer, engross your conscious self in another activity. Watch some TV, read a book, etc.

8. At the end of the session, thank whoever has communicated and shared their information with you. Touch something solid such as a chair or table to ground yourself.

- *Psychometry* -

Psychometry is my personal favorite form of divination. Psychometry is when you hold an object in your hand and receive the vibrations from it. Actually, there is no such thing as an inanimate object. Life is everywhere, in the trees, clouds, rocks, earth, and sky. We all possess the ability to do psychometry just as we do any other form of divination. Your mind is like a radio. You project thoughts and also receive thoughts the entire day. Even as you sleep your subconscious is still sending and receiving information. It is entirely possible for you to become attuned to vibrations of energy that register upon your consciousness which will enable you to describe details concerning an object and its history or even the history of its owner. When you heighten your senses, or fine-tune them, you become aware of unseen forces and vibrations invisible to our normal, everyday senses of sight and sound.

Psychometry, like any other form of psychic phenomena, is based on connecting with the individual who is attached to the object, their spirit guides and your spirit guides. All these forces are working together to create the flow of information which you receive as messages from the other side. Stop to consider that all of your basic thinking is done in pictures and symbols. You usually see things before you say them. Mental images form in your mind and you then begin labeling them with words. Words are symbols as well. Even someone that is blind from birth still has a mental image in their head before they speak.

I would suggest that when you first start practicing psychometry, have family or friends line you up with sitters that you do not know very well. This is a critical component that will greatly enhance your ability and speed at which you learn to hear and understand spirit communication. The less you know about the person you are reading for, the more you will trust the information that you hear, feel, see, sense, taste, and smell. You will have no reason not to trust the information and will give a far better and more accurate reading. Hold an article in your hand such as a ring, watch, or keys that belong to your sitter. I usually prefer someone's watch or piece of jewelry because this is a personal item and usually something they wear often and has become impressed heavily with their energy. Photographs are ideal also for psychometry. Hold the article while you meditate. Breathe in deep through your nostrils, and exhale through your mouth. Tell yourself to relax with each breath. As you quiet your mind and are in your psychic place, now receive the vibrations and impressions about the object. When you are finished meditating, rub your fingers over the object very slowly. Think of this object as having a soul and an electromagnetic energy field, an aura. Ask the soul of this article and your spirit guides to reveal something to you. You simply pause and wait for the images, sounds, words, or impressions to come to you. These will come in one or more different forms. The most important thing is to be calm, and wait for the intuitive impressions. Be receptive.

Remember, never let your mind project an answer, but simply let the answers come to you. Be clear and as precise in your descriptions as possible when relaying the information and messages to your sitter. You will be utterly amazed at the accuracy of what you receive. When you touch something or hold an object or even someone's hand, you can feel through your psychic senses impressions and validations of vibrational energy that comes in the form of thoughts, words, feelings, and visions. You are using the five C's to interpret the language of these vibrations; clairaudience, clairvoyance, clairsentience, clairalience and clairhambience. You must allow your mind to relax and be open to receiving the information. Believe and trust what you receive. If you doubt what you are getting, then you are allowing your conscious mind to get involved. Your conscious mind knows nothing about the object other than what someone told you. You can only trust what comes to you, not what comes from you. When you are finished with your session and do not feel you are receiving anything more from spirit, thank your guides for their assistance, and hand the object back to its owner. Be sure to ground yourself. All you have to do is practice, and then practice some more.

We all have this ability, and everyone can develop it. I personally have found psychometry to be one of the most effective means of learning to recognize and communicate with spirit. Please be patient with yourself and don't get discouraged if you are unable to make a connection with your loved ones or guides right away. When learning to tap into your higher consciousness and speak to spirit, you must be disciplined and patient. Raising your level of awareness, you will eventually recognize signs and symbols of your loved ones coming through. Whether it is only a one word validation, or a host of messages you receive, know that your loved ones worked very hard to get that message to you. Remain optimistic and focused in your development and the rewards will come, I promise. Be true to yourself, follow your intuition, and keep your heart and mind open to the aspects of a higher power. Be the best person you can be. Make use of your spiritual awareness to aid in the comfort and encouragement of others. Listed in the back of this book are resources I've found helpful in my journey to spiritual enlightenment. I send to you my sincerest wishes for much success in your spiritual quest.

For more information on Kathleen Tucci, her seminars, lectures, or appearance schedule, you can write her at:

Kathleen Tucci
5512 Charleston Drive
Frisco, Texas 75035

Or visit her website at www.kathleentucci.com

If you would like to submit an inspirational story, please mail it to the above address or email it to kathleen@kathleentucci.com.

Resources

- Books -

Life After Life by Dr. Raymond Moody Jr., M.D.
Hello From Heaven! by Bill and Judy Guggenheim
Tarot Plain and Simple by Anthony Louis
How To Meet And Work With Spirit Guides by Ted Andrews

- Websites -

www.compassionatefriends.org
www.after-death.com
www.ofspirit.com
www.griefcounselor.bigstep.com
www.aarp.org/griefandloss/
www.ehealingtree.com

Printed in the United States
79867LV00002B/388-399